DISPLAYING THE
GOSPEL OF GRACE

TITUS

COURTNEY DOCTOR
& HUNTER BELESS

Lifeway Press®
Brentwood, Tennessee

Published by Lifeway Press®
© 2025 Courtney Doctor, Hunter Beless
Reprinted September 2025

No part of this book may be reproduced or transmitted in any form or by any means, electronic or mechanical, including photocopying and recording, or by any information storage or retrieval system, except as may be expressly permitted in writing by the publisher. Requests for permission should be addressed in writing to Lifeway Press®; 200 Powell Place, Suite 100; Brentwood, TN 37027.

ISBN: 9798384502739
Item: 005848591
Dewey decimal classification: 227.85
Subject heading: BIBLE. N. T. TITUS--STUDY AND TEACHING \ CHRISTIAN LIFE \ GOSPEL

Unless otherwise noted, all Scripture quotations are taken from the Christian Standard Bible®, Copyright © 2017 by Holman Bible Publishers. Used by permission. Christian Standard Bible® and CSB® are federally registered trademarks of Holman Bible Publishers.
Scripture quotations marked (NIV) are taken from the Holy Bible, New International Version®, NIV®. Copyright © 1973, 1978, 1984, 2011 by Biblica, Inc.® Used by permission of Zondervan. All rights reserved worldwide. www.zondervan.com The "NIV" and "New International Version" are trademarks registered in the United States Patent and Trademark Office by Biblica, Inc.®
Scripture quotations marked (ESV) are from The Holy Bible, English Standard Version® (ESV®) Copyright © 2001 by Crossway, a publishing ministry of Good News Publishers. All rights reserved. The ESV text may not be quoted in any publication made available to the public by a Creative Commons license. The ESV may not be translated in whole or in part into any other language. ESV Text Edition: 2016.
Scripture quotations marked (NLT) are taken from the Holy Bible, New Living Translation, copyright ©1996, 2004, 2007, 2013, 2015 by Tyndale House Foundation. Used by permission of Tyndale House Publishers, Inc., Carol Stream, IL 60188. All rights reserved.

To order additional copies of this resource, write Lifeway Resources Customer Service; 200 Powell Place, Suite 100; Brentwood, TN 37027; Fax order to 615.251.5933; call toll-free 800.458.2772; email orderentry@lifeway.com; or order online at lifeway.com.

Printed in the United States.

Lifeway Resources
200 Powell Place, Suite 100
Brentwood, TN 37027

EDITORIAL TEAM, LIFEWAY WOMEN BIBLE STUDIES

Andrea Lennon
Director, Lifeway Women

Tina Boesch
Manager

Chelsea Waack
Production Leader

Mike Wakefield
Content Editor

Sarah Kilgore
Production Editor

Sarah Hobbs
Graphic Designer

Lauren Ervin
Cover Design

Table of Contents

About the Authors — 4

A Word from Courtney and Hunter — 6

Session One: Introduction — 12

Session Two: Entrusting the Gospel — 14

Session Three: Holding to the Gospel — 36

Session Four: Guarding the Gospel — 56

Session Five: Adorning the Gospel — 76

Session Six: Believing the Gospel — 98

Session Seven: Insisting on the Gospel — 120

Session Eight: Living the Gospel — 142

Endnotes — 166

Glossary — 167

Video Redemption Card — 177

About the Authors

COURTNEY DOCTOR received an MDiv from Covenant Theological Seminary and currently serves as the Director of Women's Initiatives for The Gospel Coalition. She is a Bible teacher and author of *From Garden to Glory* as well as several Bible studies including *In View of God's Mercies*, *Behold and Believe*, and *Remember Your Joy*. Courtney and her husband Craig have four children and five beautiful grandchildren.

DEDICATION

To Celena,

One of the great joys in my life has been growing together as older (me) and younger (you) women, loving Jesus, and encouraging each other to pursue knowing Him more. The line between discipler and disciplee is very blurred and I'm so grateful for all the ways the Lord has blessed me through you!

Much love,
Courtney

HUNTER BELESS is passionate about helping women and children know and love God more, especially through His Word. She has authored several children's books, founded *Journeywomen*, and is actively involved in ministry at her local church. Hunter and her husband, Brooks, have four wonderful kiddos. When they're not snuggled up reading a good book, you can find the Beless family gardening, riding bikes, or exploring the Buffalo River. Learn more about Hunter at hunterbeless.com.

DEDICATION

To my Titus 2 mentors, Meredith, Joyce, Linda, Amy, Gwen, Susie, and Courtney, So much of what I do is a result of what I've learned, received, heard, and seen in you. I am forever grateful for your investment in me.

Much love,

Hunter

A Word from Courtney & Hunter

Envision the most famous piece of art you've ever seen. Where was it located? Did you have to wander to the back of the museum or open a storage closet to see it? Probably not. Most museums put their finest artwork on display in a prominent place for all to see.

For example, the Mona Lisa is housed in the Louvre's largest room, a space big enough to welcome her many visitors. Vincent van Gogh's painting of the rolling night sky hangs on its own wall at the Museum of Modern Art in New York City. Michelangelo's famous statue of David is situated in the middle of the Galleria dell'Accademia in Florence, Italy. Why do museums display renowned artwork and sculptures this way? Because the most valuable, precious, and worthy works of art deserve to be clearly displayed.

Likewise, one of God's greatest works takes place when He creates a new heart within someone, frees them from the bonds of sin, and saves them for eternity. It's a wonder to behold. We are his new and glorious creation. In fact, Paul said in his letter to the Ephesians "we are his workmanship" (Eph. 2:10). But how do we humbly display this unmerited grace? How could we possibly showcase His mercy? The book of Titus will help us embrace the grace of the gospel, and understand how to display its work in our lives, homes, churches, and communities.

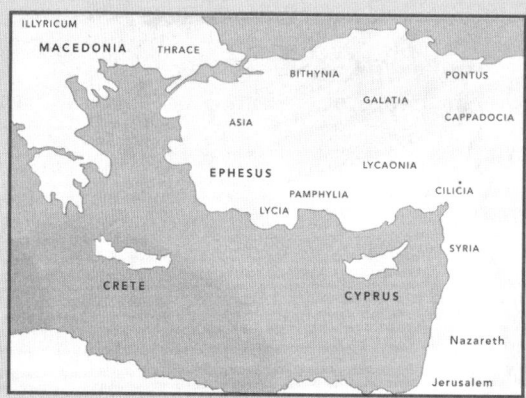

This short letter was written by Paul, a man transformed by Jesus who beautifully displayed God's life-changing grace. Paul wrote this letter to Titus, his "true son" in the faith (Titus 1:4) and trusted co-worker (2 Cor. 8:23; Gal. 2:3), charging him to insist on the gospel for the health of the church. Most likely, it was through joint missionary efforts in Crete that Paul and Titus worked together. While at some point Paul left the island, Titus remained to make sure the Cretan church was built upon the gospel of Jesus Christ. This letter was likely written in the mid-60s, around the same time as 1 Timothy. Alongside Paul's two letters to Timothy, Titus is known as a pastoral epistle because the content deals with things like church leadership, sound doctrine, and discipline. The plural benediction "grace be with all of you" that's found in Titus 3:15 also indicates that the letter, though written primarily to Titus, would also be read to the entire congregation. Furthermore, all Scripture is useful for correcting and training in the church (2 Tim. 3:16), so we will interchangeably refer to the recipients of Paul's letter as both "Titus" and "the church."

Today we still cling to the same good news Paul writes of as our only hope, both now and for all eternity. When we live according to the gospel we discover that it has the power not just to save us but also to enable us to live a godly life. Because of our salvation in Christ, we are equipped for good deeds that demonstrate His grace.

If we want to become the kind of women who know this truth, believe it, and live it out, then the message of Titus is for us. If we want to become the kind of women who love sound teaching and faithfully pass it down to others, the message of Titus is for us. If we want to become women who display the gospel through godly character and good works, the message of Titus is for us!

We hope you're convinced that the message of Titus was not just for the early church, but contains a relevant message for the church today. It is our prayer that together, we will grow in the knowledge and understanding of the truth that leads to godliness. May the Lord use our study of Titus to encourage us to know the gospel, believe the gospel, and to humbly display the gospel of God's grace.

We are truly looking forward to studying Titus together. May God powerfully meet you in the study of His Word. Our hope is that you will behold the grace of the gospel, be more transformed into the image of Jesus, and grow in grace-fueled godliness.

Much love,

Courtney & Hunter

How to Use This Study

We will be studying Titus using the inductive method—an approach that is helpful no matter what book of the Bible you study. We'll use the same series of questions each week of study to help us dig into the text. The first question will start with observation of the text by asking, *What does it say?* Then we will attempt to interpret the passage by asking, *What does it mean?* The next day we will ask, *What do other Scriptures say?* And on the last two days of our study, we will seek to apply the text by asking, *What am I to believe?* and, *Who am I to become?* We might deviate from this a bit now and then, but following this order will help us slow down and thoroughly examine the passage as we seek to properly apply its message.

What Does It Say/Observation:
When observing the passage, we want to notice things like repeated words, specific details, and any illustrations. We'll ask the basic who, what, when, where, and how questions. If you don't know the meaning of a word, look it up and write down what you learn. Also, record any questions you have as you read.

What Does It Mean/Interpretation:
With interpretation, we'll ask questions about meaning. We'll consider the intent of Paul, the author, and see the passage through the lens of the original audience—the believers in Crete who heard it first. At this point, we are not asking what this text means to *us*; we're asking what it would have meant to *them*.

What Do I Do/Application:
The last step is asking how this passage is meant to transform us. We want to consider what God has done and then ask how He wants us to respond in return. Your responses might include anything from repent, obey, believe, and pursue holiness, to wait, trust, be still, speak up, give, go, worship. We'll let the interpretation of the passage inform our application.

Every session is broken into five increments of daily study. The daily breakdown of the inductive study method is meant to serve as a guide, but there will be overlap, too. For instance, while observing the text, we might make an application in the moment. Or, while seeking to apply the text, we may need to provide interpretive context to clarify the point. Know that the categories are not hard and fast, but they will serve as general directions for our study of the book of Titus.

Plan on committing approximately twenty minutes for study each day (or an hour and half each week). Each week will start with prayer—a time for you to ask God to meet you as you study His living and active Word. We've included a prayer for each session, but we encourage you to use the space provided to journal your own prayers throughout the week. Share with God your gratitude, joy, repentance, sorrow, doubts, fears, questions, and commitments.

Though we've broken the text down into shorter passages to study each week, the letter was meant to be read in its entirety. Reading through the whole book of Titus only takes about seven minutes. We encourage you to read through the whole book at least once a week. We've included the text within your study book so you can mark it up and take notes.

Throughout this study we'll refer to different translations of the Bible. We'll use the following abbreviations to identify them.

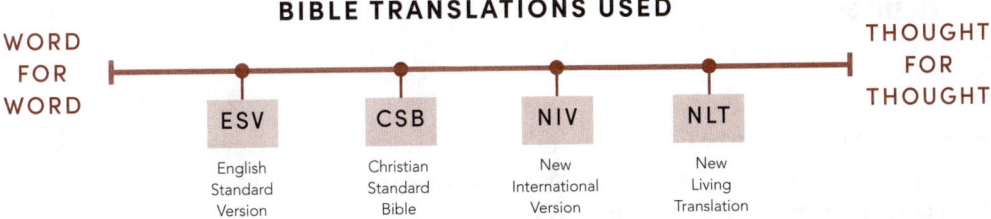

Some Other Features of the Study

DEFINITIONS

To provide insight into words and phrases you might be unfamiliar with or want more clarity about, we've included definitions in the margins of each session and a glossary of terms as an addendum on page 167.

MEMORY WORK

Titus 3:3-7 is a key section in Titus. Every week, we'll work to memorize one verse from this passage. We encourage you to take a few minutes each day of study to review the memory verse for the week by using the memory verse help we've provided. We will suggest different learning tools to help you remember the verse and access it throughout the day, but feel free to do whatever works best for your personal learning style. The discipline of hiding God's Word in your heart will bear much fruit in your life and the lives of those around you. As a bonus, you can find a Memory Verse "quiz" at lifeway.com/titus!

> [3] For we too were once foolish, disobedient, deceived, enslaved by various passions and pleasures, living in malice and envy, hateful, detesting one another. [4] But when the kindness of God our Savior and his love for mankind appeared, [5] he saved us—not by works of righteousness that we had done, but according to his mercy—through the washing of regeneration and renewal by the Holy Spirit. [6] He poured out his Spirit on us abundantly through Jesus Christ our Savior [7] so that, having been justified by his grace, we may become heirs with the hope of eternal life.
>
> **TITUS 3:3-7**

SINGING THE GOSPEL

As we learn more about who God is through His Word (theology), we should be led to worship Him (doxology). So, at the end of every week we will list a song to help us move from our study of the Scriptures to praising God in response to the glorious truths we've learned. We encourage you to sing these songs out loud and praise God with your lips, as you do so with your whole life.

FOR FURTHER READING

Throughout the study, you'll find recommended resources to help further your understanding of specific topics we cover.

TEACHING VIDEOS

You have access to teaching videos that provide additional content to help you better understand and apply what you studied in the previous week. You'll find detailed information for how to access the teaching videos that accompany this study in the back of your Bible study book.

Feel free to take notes on these teaching sessions in the space provided on the Viewer Guide pages. If you're doing this study with a group, there are questions and prompts provided on the Viewer Guide pages to help you discuss the video teaching together.

We are truly looking forward to studying Titus with you. Our hope is that you will behold the grace of the gospel, be continually transformed into the image of Jesus, and grow in grace-fueled godliness. May God powerfully meet you in the study of His Word.

You'll find detailed information for how to access the video teaching sessions that accompany this study on the card inserted in the back of your Bible study book.

Session One

Introduction

WATCH the Session One video teaching and take notes in the space below.

DISCUSSION QUESTIONS

1. What part of Courtney and Hunter's conversation resonated with you the most? Why?

2. Why is it important to study the Bible in community? Why is it personally helpful to you?

3. How does Titus fit into the big story of the Bible and why should we study it?

4. Courtney talked about how the baton of faith has been passed down through the centuries. Who passed the baton of faith on to you and how did they do so? Who do you have the opportunity to pass it on to?

5. How would you summarize the message of the gospel?

6. What context(s) do you have for living out the gospel—family, workplace, church, community, and so on?

7. When you take a moment to consider that God has placed you in your context to display the gospel of grace, what are your thoughts and emotions?

8. After hearing this opening conversation, what do you hope to get out of this study?

To access the video teaching sessions, use the instructions in the back of your Bible study book.

02

Session Two

Entrusting the Gospel

Titus 1:1-4

> ¹ Paul, a servant of God and an apostle of Jesus Christ, for the faith of God's elect and their knowledge of the truth that leads to godliness, ² in the hope of eternal life that God, who cannot lie, promised before time began. ³ In his own time he has revealed his word in the preaching with which I was entrusted by the command of God our Savior:
> ⁴ To Titus, my true son in our common faith. Grace and peace from God the Father and Christ Jesus our Savior.

Hello, and welcome to our first full week of studying Titus together! We are so excited to dive into this glorious letter with you.

As we begin, we will focus on the first four verses of this letter and consider the major themes that are introduced. But we will also peek ahead at a passage found toward the end—Titus 3:3-7. This is the passage we encourage you to memorize during the study. It is a beautiful summary of the gospel—setting it on glorious display! And it will ground us in the grace of God that leads to godliness and good works (which we will be talking about throughout this study).

MEMORY VERSE

> For we too were once foolish, disobedient, deceived, enslaved by various passions and pleasures, living in malice and envy, hateful, detesting one another.

TITUS 3:3

MEMORY VERSE HELP FOR THIS WEEK

Write Titus 3:3 on a few notecards or sticky notes and place them where you spend a lot of time—in your car, on the mirror in your bathroom, or next to the kitchen sink. You could also add Titus 3:3 to your phone wallpaper. Every time you see one of these, take a minute to recite Titus 3:3 aloud.

PRAYER
for the week

Father, You have said that Your Word is light (Ps. 119:105), power (1 Cor. 1:18), truth (2 Cor. 6:7), and life (Phil. 2:16). Help me to understand it, believe it, and align my life with it. I pray You will meet me through Your living Word and change me by its power. By Your grace, continue to conform me into the image of Your perfect Son, in whose name I pray. Amen.

DAY ONE

Observation *(What Does It Say?)*

READ TITUS 1:1-4.

We will begin every session by taking time to simply observe the passage. Good observation involves practices like reading the passage, marking repeated words, and noting verb tenses, specific information (like names and locations), the structure of the text, and contrasts or comparisons. We find it helpful to read the passage multiple times, including reading it aloud once or twice, if possible.

What were Paul's first words about . . .

- . . . God?

- . . . himself?

- . . . Titus?

What did Paul say leads to godliness?

In what do God's people hope?

With what was Paul entrusted?

How many times is the word (or concept of) *time* used? _____

- What did God promise before time began?

- When did God reveal His promise (His Word) and how does He reveal it?

Did you notice the element of time in this passage—past, present, and future? God's promise was made in the past. (In fact, it was made before time even began, but trying to comprehend that might send us on a mental spiral, so let's just stick with "in the past.") God's promise for eternal life was made in the past but will be fulfilled for all God's people in the future, when Jesus comes again and we live with him in the new heavens and new earth (Rev. 21). But that same promise, the one made long ago which will be fulfilled in the future, was accomplished in the life, death, and resurrection of Jesus at a specific time in history (~AD 33). And that promised eternal life is made available to people whenever the gospel is preached. Made before time began, fulfilled when eternal life begins, ever-present and ready to save. Who else but God can hold eternity past and eternity future together with such surety? As the psalmist said,

> Before the mountains were born
> or you brought forth the whole world,
> from everlasting to everlasting you are God.
>
> **PSALM 90:2 (NIV)**

In these opening verses, Paul referred to the gospel without saying the word "gospel" outright. He mentioned "the truth that leads to godliness" and he talked about being entrusted with something that reveals God's promise of eternal life. What is the truth that leads to godliness? What was Paul entrusted with? What is the promise that gives the hope of eternal life? It is the gospel of Jesus Christ—the good news that Jesus saves sinners like us. This is why Paul was so adamant about preaching the true gospel.

Paul began his letter to Titus by talking about the *consequences* of the gospel, rather than the *contents* of the gospel. And we're going to see that godliness and good works—both consequences of the gospel—are major themes in this letter. That's because godliness and good works should be seen in increasing amounts in the lives of those who have been saved by the gospel of grace. But, it is vitally important to know the *contents* of the gospel because the beautiful fruit of godliness and good works must have the gospel of grace as its root. Otherwise, we are just striving in our own effort. So, let's peek ahead to the end of the letter to see how Paul sets the contents of the gospel on display. As we consider the glorious gospel of grace, we will see how it fuels us to bear good fruit.

> ³ For we too were once foolish, disobedient, deceived, enslaved by various passions and pleasures, living in malice and envy, hateful, detesting one another. ⁴ But when the kindness of God our Savior and his love for mankind appeared, ⁵ he saved us—not by works of righteousness that we had done, but according to his mercy—through the washing of regeneration and renewal by the Holy Spirit. ⁶ He poured out his Spirit on us abundantly through Jesus Christ our Savior ⁷ so that, having been justified by his grace, we may become heirs with the hope of eternal life.
>
> **TITUS 3:3-7**

According to these verses, what three reasons are given for why God saved us (vv. 4-5a)?

What did *not* contribute to our salvation (v. 5)? Give an example of what these might be.

If you follow Paul's long sentence carefully, what four phrases did Paul use to communicate the way Jesus saved us?

Verse 5

-
-
-

Verse 6

-

How is each member of the Trinity involved in salvation?

What is the result of this salvation (v. 7)? Where else have you seen that phrase?

Look ahead to verse 8. What evidence shows the gospel has taken root in the life of a believer?

Draw a picture of a tree. If the tree represents your life, indicate which part of the tree represents the gospel and which part of the tree represents godliness and good works (see John 15:5).

Oh, friend, what a beautiful way to begin our study together—reflecting on the love, kindness, and mercy of God who saves sinners like us. I encourage you to begin memorizing these verses, starting with verse 3. As we hide these eternal and powerful truths in our hearts, not only will we grow in our understanding of all God has done for us, but we will also love Him more for it and be better able to share it with others. For we, like Paul, been saved by and entrusted with the glorious gospel of grace.

DAY TWO

Interpretation *(What Does It Mean?)*

READ TITUS 1:1-4.

Now that we've spent time observing the text, we can begin to ask what it means. But remember, at this point we're not asking what it means to us, we're asking what it meant to them—the original audience at the time it was written.

Why do you think Paul begins his letter by describing himself as both a servant and an apostle, and why would this have been important to the people on Crete?

APOSTLE

The New Testament primarily uses the word *apostle* to refer to the twelve disciples and Paul—men who had seen the risen Christ and been commissioned by him to preach the gospel to the ends of the earth.

According to verse 1, what is the relationship between faith, knowledge, truth, and godliness?

Restate that relationship in your own words.

What difference does the word *the* make in the phrase "knowledge of the truth"?

To the original audience, what would have been significant about God promising to accomplish salvation/eternal life before time began? (Hint: It's probably not very different from its significance for you.)

How does this impact your understanding of His love for you and your security in Him?

What do you think the phrase "the faith of God's elect" means?

How does the fact that God promised the hope of eternal life before time began inform your answer?

Paul knew he had been called to serve God by proclaiming the gospel so that people—all those whom God foreknew—would be saved. That is what he meant when he wrote, "for the sake of the faith of God's elect" (ESV).

Paul ended his greeting in verse 4 by identifying Titus as his "true son in our common faith" and wishing him the same two things he wished the recipients of all his letters—grace and peace. I love the combination of the phrases "true son" and "common faith." It seems Paul was establishing two things. First, his fatherly relationship to Titus. He was most likely older than Titus and had probably led Titus to the Lord, so Paul took his responsibility to disciple Titus seriously. This relationship would have naturally contained some authority on Paul's part. But Paul's inclusion of the phrase "in our common faith" leveled them. They were fellow sojourners, two men following Jesus. They needed equal grace, equal comfort, equal strength, and equal wisdom. They we're both entrusted with the same gospel and were being called to join God on the same mission. And, as we'll see on Days Four and Five, so are we.

As we wrap up our study today, I'd love for you to think about Paul's greeting in verse 4, "grace and peace."

Write a definition for *grace* that you think Paul would agree with. What difference does grace make in the life of a believer?

GRACE

God's unmerited favor

Grace. We will hear and use this beautiful word over and over again in this study. So, let's make sure we share a good definition of this crucial word. Grace means that God gives us, in Jesus, salvation and eternal life. The gift is unmerited and unearned. In fact, we've "earned" the opposite—God's wrath and condemnation. But, because God is full of grace, He gives us Jesus and everything we need is found in Him.

Write a definition of *peace* that you think Paul would agree with. What difference does peace make in the life of a believer?

PEACE

A complete sense of well-being in and through Christ

Biblical peace goes beyond a simple absence of conflict. Rather, it is a holistic sense of well-being that only comes through a right relationship with God through Jesus Christ. It is the knowledge and assurance that because of who Jesus is, what I have in Him, and who I am in Him, all is well, even when my circumstances seem to say differently. As the Scripture says, Jesus not only gives us His peace (John 14:27), He is our peace (Eph. 2:14-17).

Work on your memory verse and, as you contemplate who we all are apart from Jesus, let the reality of God's grace and peace wash over you.

DAY THREE

Interpretation (What Do Other Scriptures Say?)

READ TITUS 1:1-4.

CROSS REFERENCE

Another verse in the Bible that shares a similar word, topic, or theme with the verse you are reading

In order to faithfully interpret Scripture, we need to remember that the Bible never contradicts itself. That means we need to search the whole counsel of God's Word to see how other passages shed light on the one we're studying. The best way to interpret Scripture is with other Scripture. Checking cross references helps prevent us from using a verse or verses out of context. It also helps us marvel at God, who, through forty human authors and over a two-thousand-year period, has given us one cohesive, magnificent story in Scripture that holds together from beginning to end!

Paul called himself a "servant of God." On one hand, some of us would probably prefer to be called "friend of God." But on the other hand, I can't imagine a higher privilege than serving God. Was that title unique to Paul or were others called servants of God? Let's take a look.

Read Psalm 105:26 and 2 Samuel 7:8.

He sent Moses his servant, and Aaron, whom he had chosen.

PSALM 105:26

So now this is what you are to say to my servant David: 'This is what the LORD of Armies says: I took you from the pasture, from tending the flock, to be ruler over my people Israel.

2 SAMUEL 7:8

Who else is called God's servant?

Read 1 Corinthians 6:19 and Revelation 5:9.

Don't you know that your body is a temple of the Holy Spirit who is in you, whom you have from God? You are not your own.

1 CORINTHIANS 6:19

*And they sang a new song: You are worthy to take the
scroll and to open its seals, because you were slaughtered,
and you purchased people for God by your blood from
every tribe and language and people and nation.*

REVELATION 5:9

According to these passages, why should you consider yourself a servant, too?

Read John 3:36; 1 John 5:11, 13; and Colossians 3:4, and answer the following questions.

The one who believes in the Son has eternal life, but the one who rejects the Son will not see life; instead, the wrath of God remains on him.

JOHN 3:36

[11] And this is the testimony: God has given us eternal life, and this life is in his Son. . . . [13] I have written these things to you who believe in the name of the Son of God so that you may know that you have eternal life.

1 JOHN 5:11,13

When Christ, who is your life, appears, then you also will appear with him in glory.

COLOSSIANS 3:4

Who receives eternal life?	
Who gives eternal life?	
How do we receive it?	
When will we experience it?	

SESSION TWO: ENTRUSTING THE GOSPEL

Read 1 Peter 1:18-20.

He was foreknown before the foundation of the world but was revealed in these last times for you.

1 PETER 1:20

What do you learn about when salvation was planned and when it was accomplished? How is this similar to what we read in Titus 1:2-3?

God *planned* and *promised* salvation before He created a single atom. When the time came to accomplish that salvation, Jesus set aside His glory, took on flesh, and dwelt among us (John 1:1-14; Gal. 4:4-5; Phil. 2:5-8). At a specific time in history (~AD 33), Jesus, having lived a perfect life, died a sacrificial death and rose victorious from the grave. That was how salvation was accomplished. If you have believed in Jesus, you received this salvation at some point in your life. And for all of us who have received it, we look forward, with hope, for this salvation to be complete. That is the hope of glory. And every bit of it rests on the promises of God.

Read Numbers 23:19 and Hebrews 6:17-18.

*God is not a man, that he might lie,
or a son of man, that he might change his mind.
Does he speak and not act,
or promise and not fulfill?*

NUMBERS 23:19

¹⁷ Because God wanted to show his unchangeable purpose even more clearly to the heirs of the promise, he guaranteed it with an oath, ¹⁸so that through two unchangeable things, in which it is impossible for God to lie, we who have fled for refuge might have strong encouragement to seize the hope set before us.

HEBREWS 6:17-18

What do these passages testify about God's character?

What difference does this attribute make in how we understand Titus 1:1-4?

The gospel is the message of salvation. Through the preaching and proclamation of it God saves people. And, just as Paul and Titus were entrusted with the gospel in the first century, you and I are entrusted with it today. But why? Why would God trust us to be the way He brings His salvation—the one He planned, promised, and accomplished—to bear in the lives of the people around us? I have no idea. But He does.

Read Romans 10:14.

How, then, can they call on him they have not believed in? And how can they believe without hearing about him? And how can they hear without a preacher?

ROMANS 10:14

How does this verse stress the importance of proclaiming the gospel to those around you? (Note: "Preacher" can also be translated "one who proclaims." Paul is referring to anyone who shares the gospel.)

List two to three people you know who are unsaved. Prayerfully consider when and how you can proclaim the good news to them.

None of us feel adequate to the task of sharing the gospel. But if we are saved servants, we have been entrusted with the message that saved us. It's good news we must pass on. As one theologian said, "Some may preach the gospel better, but no one will preach a better gospel."[1]

Take a moment and practice reciting this week's memory verse.

DAY FOUR

Application *(What Am I to Believe?)*

READ TITUS 1:1-4.

As we've said, the Bible is meant to do more than merely *inform* us—it's meant to *transform* us. God uses His Word to conform His people more and more to the image of His Son by the power of His Spirit. This process is called sanctification, and even though it's a lifelong journey, it is a wonderful, beautiful blessing of belonging to God and growing in Him. It's what Paul was referring to when he said the knowledge of the truth leads to godliness.

Knowing the effectual work of God's Word, we should come expectantly anytime we read or study it. We should expect God to change, convict, instruct, reorient, comfort, encourage, strengthen, and transform us. We should expect Him to change not only what we do, but also what we love and how we think. Consequently, we are going to spend one day in each session thinking about what God is asking us to believe and another day asking who we, as a result, are to become.

Identify and describe two areas of your life—one negative and one positive—where what you believe dictates how you live.

In verse 1, how did Paul say knowledge impacts our living? What kind of knowledge did he say we need?

List what you might need to stop believing and what (according to our verses this week) you might need to start believing.

How would you define godliness? In what ways is your knowledge of the truth leading you into greater godliness?

If godliness involves looking more like Jesus and realizing more victory over sin, how do we increase in godliness? One of the main ways is by studying and believing God's Word, by God's grace, with the help of the Holy Spirit. That statement should be encouraging, because that's exactly what you're doing in this moment! The knowledge of the truth, as you believe it by faith, will lead to godliness and good works, and the Word of God will sanctify you through and through. This is good news!

What is your hope of eternal life? What knowledge fuels that hope? How does that hope impact how you live?

From Titus 1:1-4, list what we need to know and believe. (We've provided a couple of items to get you started).

- Knowledge of the truth leads to godliness
- God cannot lie
-
-
-

Read Titus 3:3-7 again. List some of the truths we should know and believe from these verses.

(Circle) the truths you might be struggling to believe and ask God to strengthen your faith.

Work on your memory verse today. As you do, ask God to give you more and more insight into the truth of His Word. And ask Him to transform you more and more into the image of His beloved Son.

DAY FIVE

Application *(Who Am I to Become?)*

READ TITUS 1:1-4.

We are not saved by good works, nor are we saved because we have the appearance of godliness. We are saved by God, in His mercy, grace, kindness, and love, through faith in Jesus. Paul wrote in Ephesians:

> ⁸ For you are saved by grace through faith, and this is not from yourselves; it is God's gift— ⁹ not from works, so that no one can boast. ¹⁰ For we are his workmanship, created in Christ Jesus for good works, which God prepared ahead of time for us to do.
>
> **EPHESIANS 2:8-10**

While we are not saved *by* good works, we are saved *for* good works. And we are not saved *by* godliness, but we are saved *for* godliness. Those truths dictate who we are to become: godly women full of good works.

In these first four verses, Paul made it clear our salvation is not just for our benefit. It's not just something between "me and Jesus," and it's not something that only impacts our eternal future. Our salvation is meant to impact every moment of our lives. Paul knew his purpose in life. He was a servant and an apostle who had been entrusted with the gospel message and called to proclaim it. The same is true for us.

List words that describe a servant of God. (Hint: See 2 Tim. 2:24.)

<u>Underline</u> the qualities above that describe you. ⓒircle the ones you would like God to make more true of you.

DISCIPLE (NOUN)

One who follows Jesus

DISCIPLE (VERB)

To teach and model how to follow Jesus

We've already seen that the word *apostle* is used in the New Testament primarily to refer to the men who had seen the risen Christ and been commissioned by Him to preach the gospel to the ends of the earth. But the word literally means "sent ones." In that sense, we are all apostles (just not *the* apostles), because we have all been sent by God with His message of salvation.

In what ways do you live as a "sent one"? List all the different spheres in your life (e.g. school, church, work, neighborhood, hobbies, family, etc.). Then, write specific ways you can live as a "sent one" in each of those areas.

How have you been entrusted with the gospel? By whom? Why?

FOR FURTHER READING

Growing Together by Melissa Kruger

Deep Discipleship by J. T. English

Do you, like Paul, have a true child in common faith? Do you have a younger woman in the faith (regardless of age!) that you disciple? Explain.

Discipleship is part of the life of every believer. First, every believer is a disciple, or follower, of Jesus. But there's another aspect to discipleship. The last command Jesus gave before returning to heaven was,

> All authority in heaven and on earth has been given to me. Go therefore and make disciples of all nations, baptizing them in the name of the Father and of the Son and of the Holy Spirit, teaching them to observe all that I have commanded you.

MATTHEW 28:18-20

The command in this passage is to "make disciples." *How?* As we are going (living life), we make disciples by sharing the gospel and inviting others to become followers of Jesus. We then encourage them to be baptized as a way to proclaim their transformation and identify with the community of faith. Then, the discipleship process continues by teaching them and modeling for them the Word of God so they will be able to follow Him with growing faith.

How are you being discipled? How are you involved in making disciples?

Meditate on Titus 1:1-4. Summarize it in your own words and then write a prayer of response.

Finish memorizing Titus 3:3. Spend time reflecting on what you've learned this week and jot down some takeaways. And remember, God is at work in us, through us, and for us as we study His Word!

Singing the Gospel

"My Hope Is Built / The Solid Rock" by Norton Hall Band

Session Two
VIEWER GUIDE

WATCH the Session Two video teaching and take notes in the space below.

DISCUSSION QUESTIONS

1. What part of Courtney and Hunter's conversation resonated with you the most? Why?

2. How have you seen the gospel bring people together from different walks of life? How is the gospel able to do that?

3. The gospel radically changed the purpose and trajectory of Paul's life. How has the gospel done the same in your life? In the lives of those around you?

4. Paul identified himself first as a "servant of God." Is that how you would first identify yourself? Explain.

5. How would you summarize the memory verses—Titus 3:3-7?

6. How does the memory passage help you better understand the gospel?

7. Do you ever find yourself trying to produce good works in your own power? What are the consequences of that effort?

8. God, who cannot lie, has promised us the hope of eternal life. How does God's character and His promise in this passage affect your walk with Him and witness for Him?

9. How does this passage call you to display the gospel of grace?

To access the video teaching sessions, use the instructions in the back of your Bible study book.

03

Session Three

Holding to the Gospel

Titus 1:5-9

⁵ The reason I left you in Crete was to set right what was left undone and, as I directed you, to appoint elders in every town. ⁶ An elder must be blameless, the husband of one wife, with faithful children who are not accused of wildness or rebellion. ⁷ As an overseer of God's household, he must be blameless, not arrogant, not hot-tempered, not an excessive drinker, not a bully, not greedy for money, ⁸ but hospitable, loving what is good, sensible, righteous, holy, self-controlled, ⁹ holding to the faithful message as taught, so that he will be able both to encourage with sound teaching and to refute those who contradict it.

As you read Titus 1:5-9, you might think, *So, what does this mean for me?* Hang in there. We promise that by the end of this week, you'll get it. You'll better understand the impact those who lead us spiritually can have and why character matters for them and for us.

MEMORY VERSE

> But when the kindness of God our Savior and his love for mankind appeared . . .
>
> **TITUS 3:4**

MEMORY VERSE HELP FOR THIS WEEK

Say Titus 3:4 aloud five times each day of your study. Add this verse to the notecards you made last week and continue reviewing Titus 3:3-4 as often as you can. By the end of the week, try to recite them both aloud without looking at your notes.

FOR FURTHER HELP WITH SCRIPTURE MEMORY CHECK OUT:

Read It, See It, Say It, Sing It by Hunter Beless

Memorizing Scripture by Glenna Marshall

Dwell on These Things by Natalie Abbott and Vera Schmitz

PRAYER
for the week

Father, thank You for giving me Your Word, which offers me the opportunity to know You, love You, and walk in Your ways. I confess I often struggle to obey Your commands. Give me eyes to see Your instruction clearly and soften my heart to receive it humbly. Help me to live under the authority of Your church, Your Word, and ultimately, Your Son, Jesus. I pray these things in His name. Amen.

DAY ONE

Observation *(What Does It Say?)*

READ TITUS 1:5-9.

Did you know you can read or listen to the entire book of Titus in the time it takes to brew a cup of coffee, or wash a sink full of dishes, put on your makeup, or take a shower? As you begin your study this week, take seven minutes or so to read or listen to Paul's letter to Titus in its entirety. Reading the whole book will help you better understand what Paul was communicating in each smaller portion of the letter.

What was your big takeaway from your study of Titus 1:1-4?

Take time to reread Titus 1:1-9. What connections do you see between last week's passage (Titus 1:1-4) and this week's passage (Titus 1:5-9)?

When you're telling someone something important, how do you ensure the listener understands what you're saying? If you're like me, you may tend to use the same words and phrases multiple times, in whatever way possible, to highlight your point. When I want my kids to clean their rooms, I might say, "Please, go clean your rooms. Clean up the toys, clean up the clothes strewn across the floor, and make your beds." If you only had those two sentences as a reference, you would probably get my main point—*clean*! Likewise, when we read Scripture, repeated words and phrases often help us understand the author's emphasis, which can aid our understanding of the intended message.

What repeated words do you see in Titus 1:5-9?

As we study Titus, it will be important to understand two Greek words: *presbyteros*, which is translated elder, and *episkopos*, which is translated overseer. Your church may not use these specific titles, but, throughout the New Testament, the terms elder, overseer, and pastor interchangeably refer to those who meet the qualifications listed in 1 Timothy 3:1-7 and Titus 1:5-9, teach the Word, and lead the church.

ELDER

One who oversees and manages the affairs of the local church. In Scripture, the words *elder*, *pastor*, and *overseer* are often used to reference the same office.

What title(s) does your church use to designate leadership?

According to Dr. Tim Chester, "Paul's central concern is the character, not the structure, of the leadership team–it is their role, not their hierarchy (v. 9). So, Paul's emphasis when he talks about leadership is identifying good disciples who will make good disciples."[1] No matter what terminology your church uses for those who lead, the truths of this passage are relevant and applicable for your congregation, and for you!

Where did Paul leave Titus and why did Paul leave him there?

As we discussed in Session Two, Paul's responsibility was to pass on the gospel message (Titus 1:1). He accomplished this through missionary journeys, in which he shared the gospel, planted churches, and appointed leaders. Even though Acts 27 briefly mentions his time on the island of Crete, we don't know exactly how and when the apostle and Titus were there together. What we do know is that Paul wanted Titus to make sure the Cretan church had capable leaders. So, after Paul left the island, Titus stuck around to set things in order and appoint elders in every town (Titus 1:5). Paul's focus on having strong leaders in the Cretan church shows just how important good leadership is for keeping the church healthy.

Take a quick look at the list of qualities given for elders/overseers in verses 6-9. What are some that stand out to you and why? (We'll look at the whole list more extensively tomorrow.)

Think about your church leaders. Do you know who they are? Do you pray for them? Have you ever intentionally encouraged them by naming ways you've seen them embody the gospel? As we continue our study of Titus 1:5-9 this week, it is our prayer that we will be able to answer these questions with an emphatic, *Yes!*

DAY TWO

Interpretation *(What Does It Mean?)*

READ TITUS 1:5-9.

It might be tempting to skim through this passage because it's difficult to see how it relates to us. Keep digging in, friends! Titus 1:5-9 has rich applications for all Christians.

Let's say you found an old letter in an ancestor's attic and started reading it. To understand the nuances of its meaning, it would be important to know who the author was, the location it was written from, the identity of the recipient, and where the recipient had received the letter. So, let's remember that we're reading a letter written from Paul to Titus. Before we make personal applications from their exchange, it's important to understand what Paul's message would have meant for its original recipients—Titus and the first century church in Crete. That's what we're going to do today!

> **Based on what you've studied so far, how would you summarize what Paul was communicating to Titus in verses 1:5-9?**

Yesterday, we saw that Paul left Titus in Crete, an island off the coast of Greece. When we see locations in Scripture, our eyes often glaze over, but as the mantra goes, *location is everything!* This seems to have been true for Crete. It was a strategic island that maintained harbors which served cities all over the Mediterranean Sea, making it an ideal place to carry the gospel to the ends of the earth. But there was one unfortunate detail: Cretans were notoriously violent, full of deception, and greedy (more on this next session!). As could be expected, this cultural climate was impacting the church.

> **In light of this information, why might elders like the ones Paul described be important?**

SESSION THREE: HOLDING TO THE GOSPEL

John Newton, an English minister and abolitionist in the 18th century who wrote the popular hymn "Amazing Grace," was known for living out the grace about which he sang. His home was an asylum for the perplexed and afflicted. But a nearby clergyman, Thomas Scott, often ridiculed John Newton for his traditional Christian beliefs. In contrast to Newton's godly character, Scott was known to be contemptuous and selfish.

At one point, two members of Scott's congregation became severely ill and died. True to his selfish ways, Scott didn't even visit them in their time of need. But Newton did, encouraging them with the Scriptures before their deaths. This act of kindness humbled Scott and initiated friendly conversation with John Newton. These conversations eventually led to Thomas Scott's salvation. Newton discipled Scott, and eventually left his congregation in Scott's care.

This story offers an example of what God can do through one godly leader committed to displaying the gospel of grace through his teachings, character, and conduct.

This week, our passage focuses on the importance of having godly leaders in our churches who hold to the gospel as they guide and guard their churches. Remember, Paul wrote this letter to Titus to insist on the gospel and ensure that local churches were being established well. To do this, Titus needed to put godly leadership in place that would teach sound doctrine, live it out, and silence those who contradicted it. As we'll see, the kind of character that makes this possible can only be produced by the grace of God through the transformational power of the gospel.

Paul listed several characteristics elders and overseers should display. Use the space below to list the qualifications for elders as stated in Titus 1:5-9.

Elders Must Be	Elders Must Not Be

Titus was instructed to appoint *elders* (plural) in local churches. Church leadership should not be seen as an individual undertaking, but a communal one. One person can't possibly have all the gifts necessary for building up and leading the church, nor is that burden meant to be carried alone.

It's not always possible to have multiple elders in the church, but it is something to strive for. It's also worth noting that the way shared leadership is set up won't look the same in every church. However, it is important, because shared leadership provides much-needed encouragement and accountability. It serves not only as a protection for the elders and the church but is also an example for church members as we engage in life together. It shows that the work of ministry is not limited to a select few, but something everyone can participate in. It's always better to work together rather than alone.

> **Reread verses 6-7.** Where were the elders to live out the requirements Paul listed?

The elders' godly character was to be reflected at home, among the church, and in the community. Depending on the translation you're using, it might read as though an elder's children are required to be believers. But a closer look at the context here and other passages such as 1 Timothy 3:4-5, show the expectation was for church leaders to oversee their children in a way that demonstrates they would be capable of overseeing the church.

> ⁴ He must manage his own household competently and have his children under control with all dignity. ⁵ (If anyone does not know how to manage his own household, how will he take care of God's church?)
>
> **1 TIMOTHY 3:4-5**
>
> **Why do you think it's important for the elders to embody godly character both in their homes and in the household of God?**

Paul began with these character traits because it's of primary importance that the character of our leaders be consistent both privately and publicly. The godly behavior leaders display in their households should be what they model in the household of God, and vice versa.

SESSION THREE: HOLDING TO THE GOSPEL

Review verse 9. In addition to embodying Christlike character, what else were the elders of the churches in Crete supposed to do?

What enabled the elders to encourage the church with sound teaching and refute those who contradicted it?

What was the faithful message that Paul was referring to?

The list of requirements for elders might seem overwhelming. *How can anyone consistently live out these things?* Verse 9 shows us that holding to the "faithful message" of the gospel—the message that Christ saves us by His good works, not our own—is key to elders being qualified for service in the church. As we continue our study of Titus, we'll see how important it is, not only for elders but for all of us, to hold fast to the gospel message as we seek to live it out.

DAY THREE

Interpretation *(What Do Other Scriptures Say?)*

READ TITUS 1:5-9.

Perhaps yesterday was the first time you've considered the importance of church leadership. Even now, you may be thinking, *What does this specific passage have to do with me?* It matters. Who we follow influences who we become. Paul himself encouraged the Christians at Corinth to, "Imitate me, as I imitate Christ" (1 Cor. 11:1). Like Paul, our church leaders ought to be following in Christ's footsteps and leading us to do the same. Let's look at a few other passages to better understand how our church leaders should live out these godly requirements.

Read Acts 20:28. What job requirements of an elder, overseer, or pastor are mentioned here?

Read 1 Peter 5:2-4, and fill out the chart to show the attitudes church leaders are to avoid and embody as they lead and care for the body of Christ.

"Shepherd God's flock among you . . ."	
Not . . .	But . . .
Not . . .	But . . .
Not . . .	But . . .

SESSION THREE: HOLDING TO THE GOSPEL

Elders, or church leaders, are to care for and watch over the church, much like a shepherd cares for his sheep. Shepherds know their sheep, guide them to green pastures, feed them, tend them when they're sick, and protect them. Under their shepherd's care, the sheep are safe. Likewise, elders are not to lord their position over the church, but to come alongside its members and guide them into spiritual maturity for their good (Eph. 4:11-13). Hebrews tells us that one day, church leaders will give an account for our souls (Heb. 13:17). This kind of humble church leadership can only be accomplished by looking to the Chief Shepherd (1 Pet. 5:4), who laid down His life for His sheep.

Next, read 1 Timothy 3:1-7. Compare the qualifications of elders in Titus 1:6-9 with the list you see in 1 Timothy 3:1-7 below. Circle and connect the qualifications listed exactly or synonymously in both passages. (We've done the first one as an example.)

Qualifications for elders in Titus 1:6-9	Qualifications for elders in 1 Timothy 3:1-7
Blameless	Above Reproach

46 TITUS

Only one man was capable of perfectly embodying the characteristics listed—Jesus, the only blameless, self-controlled, sensible, and righteous one. He is our chief elder, our great shepherd, and the overseer of our souls (1 Pet. 2:25). Only Jesus can qualify leaders for the task of guiding and guarding our churches in the truth of the gospel. As our leaders undertake this challenging assignment, they must rely on Christ, knowing He is the only one who makes them worthy of their role.

> How would you summarize Paul's main point in this portion of his letter? (Hint: try using the themes and ideas we saw repeated in Titus 1:5-9.)

Titus 1:5-9 shows us that for churches to be healthy and effective, they need godly elders who display Christlike character and hold to the gospel, teaching it correctly and refuting those who contradict it. As we've seen, church leadership is not a position to be authoritatively wielded over others, but one to be sacrificially and humbly stewarded in such a way that we're pointed to the most humble, sacrificial leader of all, Jesus.

Take a moment and practice reciting this week's memory verse.

DAY FOUR

Application (What Am I to Believe?)

READ TITUS 1:5-9.

It's no secret that bad leaders have wreaked havoc in the church. In recent years, there have been toxic leaders in popular ministries and prominent churches who embody everything *but* the list of qualifications we've been studying in Titus 1:5-9. As a result, it seems like more people are leaving the church than ever before. Many distrust the church and her leaders—and not without cause.

This situation grieves God. Why? Because God loves His church. And, as followers of Jesus, we are to love what God loves. The church is the bride of Christ, the one Jesus is coming back to get, and that which the gates of hell will not prevail against. So today, our hope is that Paul's words to Titus will help us examine our hearts, humbly consider what we believe, and seek to rightly align our beliefs with God's Word so that we would truly love His church.

> Before we studied this passage, what came to mind when you thought about church leadership? Review the list of words below and (circle) three words that describe your thoughts and feelings.

Respect	Fear	Revere
Resent	Love	Doubt
Trust	Frustrated	Grateful
Scared	Nervous	Admire
Apathetic	Thankful	Disappointed
At Ease	Vulnerable	Uncertain

> What personal experiences, good or bad, might be influencing your current view of church leadership?

The sad reality is that abuse happens in the church, and it is not always handled well. If you have been hurt by bad leadership in the church—either by someone abusing power, covering up wrongdoing, or failing to walk in repentance and faith—we want to say we're sorry and encourage you to seek wise counsel from a trusted pastor, godly friend, or Christian counselor. Depending on the type of abuse you've experienced, you may also need to report it to law enforcement authorities. Know that the church is supposed to be a place of safety, security, and refuge, and bad leadership has both grieved the heart of God and hurt many in His beloved church.

> Remind yourself of the kind of character and behavior godly church leaders should exemplify by reviewing the list you made on Day Two of this week's study. What difference does it make in the life of a church to have leadership like Paul prescribes in Titus?

As we discussed yesterday, no one in church leadership will live out the list of requirements perfectly, but we should expect them to consistently display godly character, hold fast to the gospel, and rely on God's grace to fulfill their calling. This is the kind of church leadership God intends. Besides people being hurt, poor leadership can result in members walking away from the church and trying to fill the void with social media, the internet, or questionable "Christian" ministries.

> Why is it often easier to follow people or ministries online instead of the leaders in our local church?

Why should we care more about following the leaders who have been prayerfully selected to oversee, lead, and protect our congregations than the people or ministries we can follow at a distance?

In our digital age, many of us devote much time to following celebrity pastors and prominent online ministries. While these ministers and resources can be a helpful supplement to our spiritual growth, we are best shepherded by people we know and who know us. Our local church leaders know our specific needs, and hopefully genuinely care about our spiritual well-being (Heb. 13:17). It's spiritually dangerous to only listen to people who say what we want to hear. Let's graciously lend our ear to the local church leaders God has given us, knowing they are for our spiritual good.

How does Hebrews 13:17 instruct us to respond to the humble leadership of our church leaders?

Our leaders are to be a picture of true discipleship—teaching and training in godliness in the context of relationship—within our local churches. In turn, we are to follow their leadership, encouraging and supporting them so that their task of leading is filled with joy.

Look back at the list of words you circled to describe your thoughts on church leadership (p. 48). Put a box around the words that express the attitude you now want to embrace when it comes to your spiritual leaders. How has studying this passage affected your thinking and attitude?

We hope you've seen how the gospel transforms our beliefs about church leadership. As we close, let's reflect on the mercy we've all—church leaders and church members alike—received in Christ by reviewing our memory verse for the week, Titus 3:5.

DAY FIVE

Application *(Who Am I to Become?)*

READ TITUS 1:5-9.

As we learned this week, Titus 1:5-9 expects much from our leaders. But it would be hypocritical to insist that our leaders embody what we do not personally prioritize. Sisters, we must believe that for churches to be healthy they need godly leaders who hold fast to the gospel. But we must also pursue godliness and hold fast to the same gospel our leaders preach and teach. Most of us lead in some capacity, whether in the church, a business, a small group, a community organization, with small children, or in some other way. So, one question we need to ask ourselves is, *What kind of character do we exhibit as leaders? Are we displaying the attributes mentioned in the passage?*

Of the list of character qualities in Titus 1:6-9, circle the ones that best describe you and box the ones you need to grow in.

Blameless	Hospitable	Righteous
Humble	Loving what is good	Holy
Patient	Sensible	Self-controlled

How does Titus encourage us to grow in this kind of godly character? (Hint: Look back at Titus 1:1.)

Make a quick list of character qualities you look for in those you follow, vote for, promote, and/or value.

How do these characteristics line up with Paul's list for church leaders? If different, how and why?

While our culture screams for independence and cringes at the idea of submission, as Christians we have the opportunity to model joyful submission to Jesus by placing ourselves under the authority of godly leaders in local churches. This doesn't mean we blindly follow what they say or never question their leadership decisions. Our leaders aren't perfect, regardless of who they are. Instead, it means we commit to listening to their teaching and walking in obedience, as long as their instructions align with Scripture. Hebrews 13:17 (NLT) says,

> Obey your spiritual leaders, and do what they say. Their work is to watch over your souls, and they are accountable to God. Give them reason to do this with joy and not with sorrow. That would certainly not be for your benefit.

We benefit when we obey God's instruction to follow godly leaders who have made it their aim to help us follow Jesus. If you are not currently a member of a local church, we hope you'll see the value of being part of a community of believers committed to Christ and the gospel of grace. Through this study of Titus, we pray you're growing in your understanding of and appreciation for leadership in the church. As we said, church leaders are not perfect, and they're not meant to dominate, harm, or control us. But by God's grace, most are very good and godly people, and we can look to them for spiritual nourishment, protection, and guidance.

How can we know, encourage, and support our church leaders as they strive to embody the character described in Titus 1:5-9?

How could supporting and encouraging the leaders in your church contribute to the overall health and culture of your church?

Use the space below to list three to four things you can do this week to support and encourage the leaders in your church.

Paul closes this section of his letter with the reminder that good church leaders are able to instruct the body in sound doctrine and rebuke those who contradict it. That's what we're going to talk about in our study next week.

Singing the Gospel

"Yet Not I But Through Christ in Me" by City Alight

Session Three
VIEWER GUIDE

WATCH the Session Three video teaching and take notes in the space below.

DISCUSSION QUESTIONS

1. What part of Courtney and Hunter's conversation resonated with you the most? Why?

2. What are some ways leadership has been identified in the churches you've attended?

3. Name a person in church leadership who has positively impacted your walk with Christ? In what way?

4. If an unchurched friend asked you why they should be involved in a local church, what would you say?

5. How have you most benefited from being part of a local church?

6. If you had just moved to a new community and were looking for a local church to attend, what characteristics would you be looking for?

7. What would you do or say to help someone work through church hurt?

8. Of the characteristics of a sound church leader listed in verses 6-9, which seem most important to you and why? Which ones seem most important for you to display as a follower of Christ? Why?

9. What are some ways you are currently supporting your church leadership? What are some other things you could be doing?

10. How does this passage call you to display the gospel of grace?

To access the video teaching sessions, use the instructions in the back of your Bible study book.

04

Session Four

Guarding the Gospel

Titus 1:10-16

> [10] For there are many rebellious people, full of empty talk and deception, especially those from the circumcision party. [11] It is necessary to silence them; they are ruining entire households by teaching what they shouldn't in order to get money dishonestly. [12] One of their very own prophets said, "Cretans are always liars, evil beasts, lazy gluttons." [13] This testimony is true. For this reason, rebuke them sharply, so that they may be sound in the faith [14] and may not pay attention to Jewish myths and the commands of people who reject the truth.
>
> [15] To the pure, everything is pure, but to those who are defiled and unbelieving nothing is pure; in fact, both their mind and conscience are defiled. [16] They claim to know God, but they deny him by their works. They are detestable, disobedient, and unfit for any good work.

While the apostle Paul was neither a mother nor a bear, the phrase "mama bear" seems an accurate description of him based on our passage this week. If you've ever seen a video (or experienced this scenario in real life!) of a person or animal crossing paths with a mother bear and her cubs, you know that the mama bear will fiercely defend her cubs. She will attack first and attack to kill. Why? Because she loves her cubs and knows she is their only line of defense.

Paul behaved like a mama bear when he saw the deadly danger of false teachers. Was he harsh in this passage? Yes. But it's because he loved the church and knew it was his job to defend her.

MEMORY VERSE

He saved us—not by works of righteousness that
we had done, but according to His mercy.

TITUS 3:5a

MEMORY VERSE HELP FOR THIS WEEK

Emphasize specific words as you read the memory verse aloud each day.

"He **saved us**—not by works of righteousness that we had done, but according to **His mercy**."

Try emphasizing different words in the verse as you read it again and again.
Here's another example:

"He saved us—not by **works of righteousness** that we had done, **but according** to His mercy."

Emphasizing different words in the verse will help it stick in your brain as you continue to repeat it throughout the week.

PRAYER
for the week

Father, I come before You and ask that You use Your Word to renew my mind and transform me more and more into the image of Jesus. Send Your Spirit to help me understand it rightly and apply it faithfully. I ask You to give me discernment to live in a way that is pleasing to You and fit for every good work You have for me. In Jesus's name. Amen.

DAY ONE

Observation *(What Does It Say?)*

READ TITUS 1:10-16.

In the previous session we saw how the lives and character of church leaders was to confirm, or be aligned with, their profession of faith. As a good friend of mine says, "Their 'do' needs to match their 'say.'" Or, as you've probably heard, your walk needs to match your talk. Paul continued that theme in this passage by contrasting those whose lives and doctrine match and those whose don't. The consistency between character and action will be a litmus test to know the difference between an instructor of sound doctrine and a false teacher.

> Briefly review the last session. According to verse 9, what two things were the overseers of the church supposed to be able to do? (Hint: The answer follows the phrase "so that.")

Our passage for this session explains why Paul needed to say, "and refute those who contradict [sound teaching]" (v. 9).

> According to verses 10-11, answer the following:
>
> - How did Paul describe the teachers who contradict sound doctrine?
>
> - How did he describe their teaching?
>
> - What did he say needed to be done to these false teachers?

- Why? What was Paul's primary concern?

- What did Paul say motivated these people?

Paul was zealous to protect those in the church. We can understand that. But the next two verses sound awful to our modern ears. It seems Paul was condemning with a broad brush an entire group of people by his agreement with this statement: "Cretans are always liars, evil beasts, and gluttons" (v. 12). Yikes.

There are two things we need to know. One, Paul was most likely quoting a Cretan poet, Epimenides, who had lived over six hundred years prior to Paul writing this letter.[1] So, Paul was quoting what another Cretan said about his own people. Two, Paul had just finished telling Titus to appoint elders, *Cretans*, who were blameless, humble, calm, kind, generous, hospitable, sensible, righteous, holy, and self-controlled. So, clearly Paul did not think that all Cretans were dishonest, evil, and gluttonous! Paul was using strong rhetoric to make a strong point.

Read verses 13-14. For what reason did Paul want Titus to rebuke these false teachers? What was Paul's ultimate aim?

Paul wanted these false teachers to be "sound in the faith," to be restored—knowing the gospel, believing the gospel, teaching the gospel, and living the gospel. Paul's harshness was a form of grace, and he was modeling for Titus what he instructed Titus to do—rebuke them sharply. In fact, many of Paul's letters contain this same attitude of boldly calling out false teachers (i.e., in Galatians, Paul says that false teachers should emasculate themselves!). Later in this session we'll discuss when and why a rebuke like this might be necessary.

Read verse 15. What two adjectives did Paul use to describe the false teachers?

What aspects of their lives did it cloud?

What three adjectives did Paul use to describe the false teachers in verse 16?

Paul clearly noted the importance of consistency between someone's claim to know God and the "works" they did. For the false teachers, the two things didn't line up. In other words, their "do" didn't match their "say." This inconsistency prompted Paul's harsh rebuke.

Brennan Manning famously said, "The greatest single cause of atheism in the world today is Christians: who acknowledge Jesus with their lips, walk out the door, and deny Him by their lifestyle. That is what an unbelieving world simply finds unbelievable."[2] There is great damage done when Christians have a large gap between their profession of faith and the way they live their lives.

The need for consistency between what we profess and how we live isn't important just for church leaders. It's vital for all of us. As you study this week's passage, consider whether those closest to you would say there is consistency between what you profess and how you live. Ask God to show you where that gap needs to close. There are probably few prayers the Lord delights to answer more!

DAY TWO

Interpretation *(What Does It Mean?)*

READ TITUS 1:10-16.

Today we will focus on what this passage meant to the original audience. Why did Paul write these words to Titus? Remember, the church was in her infancy—probably only thirty years or so after the death and resurrection of Jesus. And Paul's inner mama bear was going to defend these young churches against any and all harm.

Paul seems to have two main concerns—the character of the teacher and the content of the teaching.

> From this passage, list the characteristics of both the teacher and the teaching Paul was concerned about.

Teacher	Teaching

Paul gave some clues in these verses that indicate the type of false teaching He was most concerned about.

> **Verse 10 tells us that these false teachers were "from the circumcision party" (meaning they were Jewish people who had converted to Christianity). What kind of false teaching might they have been promoting?**

> **What else do we learn about their teaching in verse 14? What do you think each of those phrases might mean?**

Most likely, the false teaching in Crete centered around what we can call a "Jesus + Something" theology. This happens whenever someone adds something to the requirement of salvation. The true gospel message proclaims that Jesus, and Jesus alone, saves us. It is only through His perfect life, substitutionary death, and victorious resurrection that someone can be saved. This salvation is only obtained through faith, simply believing that you need a Savior and you can't save yourself, but that Jesus did everything necessary to save you. When "you confess with your mouth that Jesus is Lord and believe in your heart that God raised him from the dead, you will be saved" (Rom. 10:9)!

Jesus + Something theology says, "Yeah, that's all true, but in order to be saved you also need to do things such as: good deeds for others, obtaining a certain amount of knowledge, believing all the "right" doctrines, giving enough money, and so forth." Paul knew that Jesus + Something teaching ruins churches, entire households, and individual believers.

> **Have you ever heard someone teach a Jesus + Something theology? If so, what was that person adding to the true gospel message?**

> **What damage can a Jesus + Something theology do to:**
> - **A believer**
>
> - **An unbeliever**

- A church

- A household

In light of these kinds of consequences, why was it so important to appoint elders who were able to "encourage with sound teaching and to refute those who contradict it" (v. 9)?

Paul was concerned not only with what was being taught, but also with the character of the person teaching. In agreeing with the harsh quote from Epimenides, Paul was saying these false teachers were dishonest, greedy, and slothful. The problem was not only preaching a dishonest gospel, but preaching the gospel dishonestly.

How might someone preach the gospel for greedy gain?

How might someone preach the gospel in sloth (or laziness)?

Why do both of these matter?

We might feel discouraged thinking about all the times and places a false teacher has taught a false gospel or taught the real gospel dishonestly. But take heart, sound churches with sound doctrine and sound leaders have been present in every age for the past two thousand years, and will continue until Jesus returns. This a testimony to the truth that God is zealous to guard His church!

DAY THREE

Interpretation *(What Do Other Scriptures Say?)*

READ TITUS 1:10-16.

Welcome back! We're eager to look at other Scriptures with you to help us understand Paul's message to Titus and why Paul was so zealous about it. Remember, the focus of the passage is that false teachers and false teaching are extremely dangerous to the church, both then and now.

> Read the following passages and answer the questions. Write what you learn about false teachers, false teaching, the harm both can cause, and what we are to do about it.
>
> - Matthew 7:15. According to Jesus, what did Jesus tell us to do about false teachers?
>
> - Acts 20:28-30. Why were people distorting the truth? What are we to do about it?
>
> - 1 Timothy 6:3-5. List the attributes of the person who teaches a false gospel (v. 4). What is the result?
>
> - 2 Timothy 3:1-5. List how false teachers in the last days are described. Again, what are we to do?

One of the most dangerous teachings in Jesus + Something theology is one that says you need to add good works as a basis for salvation. Many people believe in some form of this false gospel:

- that their eternal salvation rests on whether their good deeds outweigh their bad
- that they need to "get their lives together" before they can come to church
- that Jesus would love them (or love them more) if they were "better people"

SESSION FOUR: GUARDING THE GOSPEL

Each of these is grievously wrong.

> **Read Philippians 3:4-9.** Where do you see Paul pushing away from a Jesus + Something theology (what could he have "added" to the gospel) and how does he describe the true gospel? Write verse 9 in your own words.

Look at Titus 1:10-16. Not only were the false teachers teaching wrong content, their motivation for teaching it was wrong. Paul wrote in verse 11 they were "teaching what they shouldn't in order to get money dishonestly." They were not preaching a pure gospel nor were they preaching from a pure heart.

> **Read 1 Timothy 5:17.** Describe the difference between the church leaders Paul was referring to in Titus 1:10-16 and the teachers he was describing in 1 Timothy 5.

> How are we to care for the good leaders?

Godly church leaders are a gift to the church. Paul said they are worthy of "double honor"—respect and remuneration. We should pray for them, encourage them, and financially support them. Consider how your presence in the church could also be a gift to them. If you are in a church with godly leaders, take time this week to encourage them—simply send an email or a note, share a word of encouragement, give a small gift, or offer a prayer.

As you work on your memory verse, thank God for the mercy that has saved both you and the leaders of your church.

Take a moment and practice reciting this week's memory verse.

DAY FOUR

Application *(What Am I to Believe?)*

READ TITUS 1:10-16.

Perhaps you've wondered this week, "What in the world does this passage have to do with me?" Remember that what Paul wrote in 2 Timothy 3:16 is true:

> ***All Scripture*** *is inspired by God and is profitable for teaching, for rebuking, for correcting, for training in righteousness (emphasis mine).*

There are several profitable things from this passage for us to glean and apply in the twenty-first century!

First, false teachers have always been a problem in the church, but in this age of social media, false teaching can scroll past our eyes constantly. Though it might be subtle at times, it too easily makes its way into our hearts. Therefore, we need to be women who know and believe the gospel of grace.

At the same time, we live in the age of cancel culture where the term "false teacher" is thrown around like popcorn at a slumber party. We need to be diligent students of God's Word so that we can know the truth of the gospel, which matters are primary to the gospel, and which matters are okay to have differences of conviction on.

Primary issues are beliefs and doctrines considered essential to orthodox faith. These include but are not limited to the following:

- Salvation is by grace alone, through faith alone, in Christ alone;

- The Bible is the inerrant, infallible, inspired word of God;

- Jesus was born of a virgin and existed on earth as fully man and fully God;

- Jesus was bodily resurrected from the dead;

- The Trinity—God exists as three-in-one.

> **ORTHODOX**
>
> At its core, the word means *right belief.* Orthodoxy consists in the historical faith, summarized in the early creeds like the Apostles' Creed and the Nicene Creed.

To deny any of these is to deny the historic and orthodox Christian faith. Anyone who teaches contrary to these should rightly be called a false teacher.

Secondary issues are beliefs or doctrines that are important, but not essential, to faith in Christ. In other words, we can disagree on issues such as:

- how we view the end times and return of Christ
- when someone should be baptized (as an infant or on profession of faith)
- the method of baptism (immersion or sprinkling)
- the length of time God took to create the world
- spiritual gifts
- the role of women in church leadership

The views on these issues are usually well-studied and deeply held, regardless of which side you take. And, as with the first list, this list is not exhaustive. But none of them are essential for salvation. So, we can (and even should) believe strongly about these, but we do not call someone who holds a different conviction a false teacher.

There are also theological issues we call *tertiary*, meaning "of third rank."[3] These issues are nowhere near essential to the faith (even though some people act as if they are!). There is much freedom and liberty in issues like drinking alcohol in moderation, style of worship, the right to bear arms, political affiliation, and educational choices for our children.

Why is it helpful to consider our doctrines, beliefs, and preferences in these categories?

Are there any of your held beliefs that need to shift categories? If so, which ones?

Read Romans 14:1-5, 13-20. How does this passage address primary, secondary, and tertiary issues? What does verse 20 mean?

Why is it important to extend charity to our brothers and sisters who hold different convictions in secondary and tertiary elements of our faith?

These are not easy matters. They require that we grow in both knowledge and the ability to apply what we have learned. They require that we rely on the Holy Spirit to grant us insight, discernment, charity, wisdom, and humility.

And now, a final profitable thing from this passage. Social media has made the pathway for someone to be a teacher/influencer shorter and smoother than ever before. But, if we want to be women who teach others, we must be women who are committed to a lifetime of study—that we would know, believe, and proclaim the pure gospel.

Review Titus 3:3-7, and write down the essential elements of the gospel.

Some of the last words in all of Scripture are,

> ¹⁸ I testify to everyone who hears the words of the prophecy of this book: *If anyone adds to them*, God will add to him the plagues that are written in this book. ¹⁹ And *if anyone takes away* from the words of the book of this prophecy, God will take away his share of the tree of life and the holy city, which are written about in this book (emphasis mine).
>
> **REVELATION 22:18-19**

Using the chart below, list two to four things that might be added to the gospel and two to four things that might be taken away.

Added	Taken Away

If you are a follower of Jesus, part of the call on your life is to know the Word of God. Through His Word we will learn and grow in our understanding of who God is, how He works, and what He is doing—not just in our individual lives, but in the world. As we grow, we are to more closely align our lives, minds, and hearts with the truth. So, as you work on your memory verse, thank God for the gospel truths you see and ask Him to make you a woman who knows, believes, and can rightly divide the Word of truth.

DAY FIVE

Application *(Who Am I to Become?)*

READ TITUS 1:10-16.

If yesterday we asked the question, *what am I to believe*, today we ask, *then who am I to become*? We are to become women able to recognize a false teacher and know what to do about it. And we should be women able to teach others well. Both only happen as we know, believe, apply, and live the gospel.

> How confident are you in your ability to recognize a false teacher? What might help you grow in this important skill?

> How confident are you in your ability to share the gospel? What might help you grow in this important skill?

We've seen that false teachers not only teach a false gospel, most of them also have a gap between what they profess and how they live. Now, at some level, we all have a gap—none of us perfectly live out the reality of our faith every moment of every day. And all of us who are saved by Jesus will spend the rest of our lives closing that gap. It's called *sanctification,* and it's both a work of God and one we participate in. Salvation belongs to God alone, but after we're saved we are called to grow spiritually to become more and more like Jesus.

SANCTIFICATION

The lifelong process of being increasingly conformed to Jesus's righteousness through the work of the Holy Spirit

> Where do you see a gap between what you profess and how you live? What do you think is causing that gap?

> What steps should you take to close it? (Hint: The first step should be prayer!)

What closes the gap the quickest and most effectively is not just greater knowledge, but a deeper relationship. That's why prayer and attention to Scripture are so important. We need to consistently talk with and listen to the Lord, to pour our hearts out in prayer and hear Him speak. The main way He speaks to us is through His Word. We need to study the Bible more. We need to believe the Bible more. And we need to obey the Bible more.

As we pray and engage with Scripture, our relationship with God deepens. And as the relationship deepens the gap will begin to close. The words that come out of our mouths will start to change. They will be kinder, humbler, more patient, and more encouraging. The thoughts that run through our head will change. The things we do, the places we go, the ways we act, react, and feel will all change. The process of sanctification impacts all of who we are because we are being transformed more and more into the image of Jesus. As that happens the gap between what we profess and how we live closes. We will experience change that is deep, real, and lasting.

In our passage this week, we saw the danger caused by a Jesus + Something theology. Truth be told, bits and pieces of a Jesus + Something theology can easily creep into our beliefs. We can all fall prey to the lie that God loves us more when we are "good," or that we need to get our lives cleaned up before Jesus can save us. One of the most tragic parts of this theology is that it can push someone to lead a moral life, but never lead that person to eternal life.

> Paul pushed away from anything other than Jesus as his righteousness and salvation (Phil. 3:4-9). What part of a Jesus + Something theology might you be tempted to believe? How do you push away from it?

Considering our discussion yesterday on the differences between primary, secondary, and tertiary issues, are you more prone to rebuke someone too quickly or offer charity when a rebuke might be necessary?

How did Titus 1:10-16 help you know the difference?

Are you more prone to add something to God's Word (i.e., be a good person, get your life together, do good deeds) or take away from God's Word (e.g., dismissing essentials of the faith or ignoring certain commands)?

The Word of God is not a buffet of ideas where we can pick what we like and pass on what we don't. Neither is it a grocery list that we can add items to whenever we desire. It is the complete, sufficient, closed, perfect, and inspired Word of God, and we are to take it exactly as it is. No more, no less.

As we wrap up, we want to address our sisters who have been hurt by false teachers. We hope you found great comfort in Paul's "mama bear" approach to them. He knew the damage they could cause and came out against them. Even more than that, we hope you saw Jesus's ferocity against false teachers. The Lamb of God, who takes away the sins of the world, is also the roaring Lion, who will protect and defend His church. If you have been hurt by a false teacher in the church, Jesus sees, He cares, and He will one day make all things right.

In the meantime, while we all wait for that glorious day, may we be women saturated in the true gospel of grace, able to discern, teach, and live it out in wisdom, strength, and humility.

Singing the Gospel

"There is One Gospel" by City Alight

Session Four
VIEWER GUIDE

WATCH the Session Four video teaching and take notes in the space below.

DISCUSSION QUESTIONS

1. What part of Courtney and Hunter's conversation resonated with you the most? Why?

2. How would you define Jesus + Something theology? Do you think you could recognize it if someone you were listening to was teaching or espousing it? Explain.

3. How is it possible for us to say we don't hold or teach Jesus + Something theology, yet sometimes fall into the trap of living that way?

4. Do you think we have false teachers in our midst? Explain. How can we know when someone is a false teacher?

5. Though we are opposed to false teaching, is it possible for us to still allow it into our lives? If so, how? What might be evidence we're allowing false teaching to influence us? How do we silence the false teaching we're listening to?

6. Explain what is meant by the term "tiered theology"? Why is it essential that we agree on primary issues?

7. What are possible consequences to the body of Christ if we make it a test of fellowship for everyone to agree on secondary or tertiary issues?

8. How does getting a grasp on tiered theology help us understand that just because someone disagrees with us does not mean they are a false teacher or embracing falsehood?

9. How does this passage call you to display the gospel of grace?

To access the video teaching sessions, use the instructions in the back of your Bible study book.

05

Session Five

Adorning the Gospel

Titus 2: 1-10

> ¹ But you are to proclaim things consistent with sound teaching. ² Older men are to be self-controlled, worthy of respect, sensible, and sound in faith, love, and endurance. ³ In the same way, older women are to be reverent in behavior, not slanderers, not slaves to excessive drinking. They are to teach what is good, ⁴ so that they may encourage the young women to love their husbands and to love their children, ⁵ to be self-controlled, pure, workers at home, kind, and in submission to their husbands, so that God's word will not be slandered. ⁶ In the same way, encourage the young men to be self-controlled ⁷ in everything. Make yourself an example of good works with integrity and dignity in your teaching. ⁸ Your message is to be sound beyond reproach, so that any opponent will be ashamed, because he doesn't have anything bad to say about us. ⁹ Slaves are to submit to their masters in everything, and to be well-pleasing, not talking back or ¹⁰ stealing, but demonstrating utter faithfulness, so that they may adorn the teaching of God our Savior in everything.

Apart from Christianity, almost every other world religion can be characterized as a "do-something-to-get-something" religion. Regardless of the promised rewards—reincarnation, nirvana, or worldly possessions—they must be earned. Do enough good deeds, give enough money, perform all the right rituals, or go on all the right pilgrimages, and *then* the reward will be yours.

But Christianity is the reverse. The good news of the gospel is that Jesus did everything required to earn our salvation for us, and the only thing we must do is receive it. Then, and only then, are we able to live out what we believe. We can live faithful and fruitful lives—not to earn our salvation, but as a result of it.

This right ordering of the Christian life can be summarized in several ways:

Doctrine → Duty
Belief → Behavior
Orthodoxy → Orthopraxy
Know → Do

Indicatives → Imperatives
Relationship → Response
Sound teaching → Sound living

Our next two sessions highlight this reality. But instead of Paul leading with the first column (doctrine, belief, indicatives), he leads with the second column (duty, behavior, imperatives). As we study Titus 2:1-10, remember the behavior Paul called for is only possible because of what he said in verse 11, "For the grace of God has appeared, bringing salvation." This gospel message is at the heart of Paul's teaching and has implications for every season of life, as we'll see in our text today.

MEMORY VERSE

> He saved us—not by works of righteousness that we had done, but according to his mercy—through the washing of regeneration and renewal by the Holy Spirit.
>
> **TITUS 3:5**

MEMORY VERSE HELP FOR THIS WEEK

Emphasize the words in bold as you read our memory verse aloud five times each day:

"He **saved** us—not by works of **righteousness** that **we** had done, but according to his **mercy**—through the washing of **regeneration** and **renewal** by the Holy Spirit."

SESSION FIVE: ADORNING THE GOSPEL

PRAYER
for the week

Father, Your instruction is perfect, renewing our lives (Ps. 19:7). Your precepts are right, making our hearts glad (Ps. 19:8). Help me come to Your Word with humility, receive it as my ultimate authority, and obey it with gladness. Thank You for the way Your Word helps me to know Jesus and live more like Him. I pray these things in His name. Amen.

DAY ONE

Observation *(What Does It Say?)*

READ TITUS 2:1-10.

Whether it's the latest designer bag, a document you receive in the mail, or someone's personality, we all love the real deal. But how do you determine the difference between an authentic and a fake? When it comes to money, for example, counterfeit experts are trained to spot counterfeit bills not by studying copycats, but by studying the real thing. They examine, touch, and even smell actual dollar bills, so that when they get a whiff of a fake one, they know it instantly. This week we're going to focus on authentic gospel teaching and authentic gospel teachers—so we will be better able to know, believe, trust, and proclaim the real deal.

We discussed the danger of false teaching within the church in Session Four. We saw how, when things are added to or taken away from the gospel, entire households can be ruined, along with the church's witness. In contrast to false teaching that results in ungodliness, Paul encouraged Titus to prioritize sound teaching that would produce true, godly believers within the church.

Though the culture in Crete was self-serving, the church was to be marked by a shared purpose to display the good news of the gospel. They were to be marked by counter-cultural relationships, including relationships that spanned generations. As Paul unpacked what intergenerational gospel-living looks like, he addressed five different categories of Christians, revealing that God uses people in every season of life to accomplish His mission in the church.

SOUND

Healthy, whole, fully functioning, not broken

Paul's instructions to slaves in verses 9-10 weren't intended to endorse the practice of slavery, but to humanize and dignify Christians who found themselves bound in it. Paul wasn't speaking to the moral issue of slavery in this passage, though perhaps many of us wish he would have. Instead, he wrote to encourage Christian bondservants to reflect the transforming power of the gospel through their interactions with their masters. This action, once again, would show that people in every station of life—even those not seen as valuable in the broader culture—have immense value in the kingdom of God.

Number the different groups of Christians that Paul mentions in the order in which Paul mentions them.

Slaves

Younger Women

Older Men

Younger Men

Older Women

What characteristics did Paul prescribe for each group of people in the church?

Older Men	Older Women	Younger Women	Younger Men	Slaves

When we look at a list of character qualities to be displayed in believers, it's tempting to immediately strive to apply them in our lives. As much as we want the Word to bring lifestyle change, it's important to move slowly and take time to understand Paul's message for his original audience. This patience helps us rightly interpret the passage and rightly apply it.

We need to remind ourselves that Paul wrote this letter to Titus, and it was to be shared with the church in Crete. As faithful readers, our job is to pull out the principles—the eternal truths God has for us—while allowing the specific practices to be contextualized in every century, every continent, and every culture. So, as we move forward and consider the outcomes of Paul's guidance, we must keep in mind that the list he offered was not exhaustive.

Draw a line to connect the appropriate "so that" statements with the result we find in the text. Note: your translation might use a different transitional word or phrase like, "and so," or, "then," instead of, "so that."

So That Statement	Result
Older women are to . . . teach what is good, so that (v. 4)	they may adorn the teaching of God our Savior in everything
Older women are to . . . love their husbands and children, be self-controlled, pure . . . so that (v. 5)	any opponent will be ashamed, because he doesn't have anything bad to say about us
Your message is to be sound beyond reproach, so that (v. 8)	they may encourage the young women
Slaves are to submit to their masters in everything . . . demonstrating utter faithfulness, so that (v. 10)	God's word will not be slandered

Great work, sister! You've done an excellent job observing the text. Tomorrow, we'll take the pieces we've uncovered and combine them to help us see the big picture—to get the main idea of the text. This will help us understand how the truths of the passage impact our thoughts, actions, and life together in the local church.

SESSION FIVE: ADORNING THE GOSPEL

DAY TWO

Interpretation *(What Does It Mean?)*

READ TITUS 2:1-10.

Do your eyes glaze over when you see the word *doctrine*? Perhaps the word musters up mental images of huge books written by stodgy-looking authors who lived centuries ago. But sound doctrine isn't just about filling our heads with static knowledge. It's about filling our lives with true scriptural teaching, meant to flow from our hearts to our hands as we live it out. Sound doctrine should drive our devotion to the Lord Jesus Christ and to our brothers and sisters in the local church. Sound doctrine is the only true foundation for sound living.

> **DOCTRINE**
>
> Teaching that aligns with Scripture and results in godly living

Paul used the word *sound* three times in Titus 2:1-10: sound teaching (v. 1), sound in faith (v. 2), and sound beyond reproach (v. 8). Remember, *sound* means, "healthy, whole, functioning, not broken." Paul's repetition of this word indicates its importance. In an oral culture, repetition was used to emphasize an idea, much like we might underline or italicize a word in our writing today. Notice that "sound teaching," which can also be translated "sound doctrine," is listed first.

Why do you think Paul's instruction to proclaim sound teaching came first (2:1)?

Paul started with sound teaching because he wanted it to undergird everything in the church. He knew that Scripture-rich teaching would produce authentic followers of Christ that displayed the gospel of grace. That is what the Bible does! It is living and effective (Heb. 4:12). It is profitable for teaching, for correcting, and for training in righteousness (2 Tim. 3:16). It is a lamp to our feet and a light to our path (Ps. 119:105). God's Word helps us understand who God is, who we are in light of Him, and how we ought to live as a result.

If you're thinking, "This sounds familiar," you're absolutely right! Paul said earlier that the knowledge of the truth (sound doctrine), leads to godliness (sound living) (Titus 1:1). He also spent time listing the character qualifications of church leaders, including a charge for them to encourage the flock with sound doctrine and to rebuke those who contradict it (1:6-9). Then, he followed it with a real time situation Titus needed to deal with. Needless to say, Paul emphasized sound doctrine to Titus and the church in Crete. He knew good doctrine that leads to godly living would prove to the watching world that the gospel really was good news.

> What members of the church did Paul have in mind when he made these lists?

Paul had every member of the church in view when he penned this portion of his letter. Older and younger, in the home and outside of it, wherever they were, however they could, the church was designed to display the beauty of the gospel through life together. That, friends, is true discipleship.

The church is to teach and train its members in godliness. If we summarized the purpose of the list of instructions Paul gave the church in this section, we would probably use that exact word—godliness. It might be tempting to make the list of godly characteristics our focus, especially if you're a list-making, "Let's do this!," kinda gal. Hear us again: *it is excellent and essential to apply Scripture to our lives*, but as we do, we have to make sure our focus is rightly oriented on the One who produces godly living in us, *not* the desired outcome. Too often, we fixate on doing or being better in our own efforts, which makes us the center instead of Christ. We must resist the urge to place godly living at the center of our sound doctrine and keep Christ in His proper place at the center. He alone is worthy, and He alone enables us to live it out.

DISCIPLESHIP

Teaching and training in godliness in the context of relationship

> **Review Titus 2:1-10 again.** Summarize the character and actions to be displayed by the believers on Crete.

> For what purpose did Paul call them to this kind of godly living?

Thousands of years have passed since Paul wrote to Titus, but his words still remind us that true gospel teaching produces intergenerational gospel living that glorifies God.

> As we close, consider the season of life you're in and the calling of God in your life. Where does God have you and why? What fills your days? How are you displaying the gospel of grace in your spheres of influence? What do your relationships look like within your church body? Jot some thoughts down in the space provided. Then ask the Lord to help you receive every season with gratitude and gladness, so you can be an active, influential participant in the compelling, counter-cultural community of the church.

DAY THREE

Interpretation *(What Do Other Scriptures Say?)*

READ TITUS 2:1-10.

Sometimes we hear Christians say some version of, "I don't need the church. I just need Jesus." We need to remember that while our relationship with Jesus is deeply personal, He didn't come just to save us individually, but to rescue a people for Himself. When God draws us to Himself through his Son, we're adopted into a family of brothers, sisters, mothers, and fathers. That speaks to why Paul referred to Titus as his "true son in our common faith" (Titus 1:4). Like a healthy family, we should love one another, instruct one another, and encourage one another to persevere in our faith as we journey alongside one another until we make it all the way home.

In the family of God, one of the most helpful ways we instruct each other is through God's Word, or to put it Paul's way, "to proclaim sound teaching" (2:1). This exhortation isn't just for the pastors and preachers, but for all of us. As we proclaim, teach, and train one another in God's Word, we grow in our love for Him and help others do the same. Today, we'll explore several passages to better understand why sound teaching helps us know and love God more.

> Let's look at Paul's first letter to Timothy to gain a deeper understanding of what he meant when he said, "proclaim things consistent with sound teaching" (Titus 1:1). **Look up 1 Timothy 6:3** and fill in the following blanks.
>
> Sound teaching aligns with the teachings of _____
>
> and promotes _____.

This helps us answer the question we asked at the beginning of the week, "How can we tell the difference between false teaching and sound teaching, or an authentic and a fake?" To determine genuine Christian teaching, we must test whether or not it aligns with the words of Jesus and produces people who look like Him.

SESSION FIVE: ADORNING THE GOSPEL

Let's look at what Jesus said about the Scriptures. **Turn to Luke 24:27.** Who did Jesus say the whole Bible is about?

We don't love sound doctrine simply to know more about the Bible, to do better, or to be better. We love sound doctrine because it helps us see and treasure Jesus and live lives that reflect Him. When we study, read, and teach the Bible, we are drawing near to Jesus! It's been said that Christians are "people of the Book," and while that's true, we are also, "people of the Person—Jesus Christ." Because we love Jesus, we spend time with Him through His Word and live in a way that points others to Him. And because we love Jesus, we study sound doctrine, which is found in God's Word, to know Him better.

Read 2 Timothy 4:3-5. How does this affirm the urgency and importance of prioritizing sound doctrine?

This sounds like a description of our current age, doesn't it? In the broader culture, most people no longer acknowledge objective truth and instead cling to "their truth." Even in the church, some people want to use Scripture simply to validate their personal beliefs. As a whole, it seems we've become more interested in finding a church that conforms to our ideas as opposed to prioritizing true, biblical teaching that helps us conform to God's ideas about who we are and how we should live. It's a tragedy, because moving away from true, biblical teaching means we are moving away from Christ. Christ is the central figure of Scripture, and He should be at the center of all we do.

In **1 Corinthians 11:1**, Paul offered a tangible example of what it looks like to disciple others in the faith. What was his instruction and what does that say about how we should welcome others to follow us?

Paul encouraged the church to follow him as he followed Christ because he knew the Christian life was all about Jesus. True discipleship doesn't just offer tips about how to practice hospitality, manage our calendars, or implement a budget (though those are all good things). True discipleship centers around knowing and loving Jesus Christ and producing people that increasingly look like Him.

Whether you're at the beginning stages of knowing and loving God and his Word, or you've been devoted to Him for decades, every believer—no matter what age or stage of maturity—has a vital role to play in Christian discipleship. Tomorrow, we'll see that in every season, we live out our part by clinging with both hands to the Word of God and encouraging those around us to do the same.

Take a moment and practice reciting this week's memory verse.

DAY FOUR

Application *(What Am I to Believe?)*

READ TITUS 2:1-10.

With her palm planted firmly on the cover of her Bible, my mentor locked eyes with me (Hunter) and said, "This is no empty word for you, but your very life." Here's the thing, she didn't just quote a portion of Deuteronomy 32:47 to inspire me, she lived it out in front of me. This precious older sister consistently spent time in the Word, talked about its truths, strove to walk in obedience, and encouraged me (and everyone around her) to do the same.

Like most twenty-somethings, I asked questions like, "What job should I pursue?" "How should Christians date?" and "What should I do with my life?" While I'm sure my mentor had good insight into my inquiries, she didn't solely offer her advice. Rather, she guided me to God's Word. In doing so, this older saint taught me to go to Scripture for everything! She was convinced that God works through His Word in the hearts of His people.

> **We pointed out earlier that in his instructions to the church, Paul led with sound teaching (2:1). What are we sometimes more prone to lead with in discipling others?**

In any discipleship relationship, there's a temptation to draw women to ourselves by centering the conversation around us—our knowledge, our experiences. Instead of guiding them to the Word, we answer questions based on what we've gone through. Instead of emphasizing principles grounded in Scripture, we hone in on practical tips that have worked well for us.

One danger with this approach is that we all live in different contexts, with different callings. Each of us has unique responsibilities, personalities, families, and capabilities. While personal experience is a valuable part of discipleship, we must remember that God's Word is the most helpful thing we can offer one another.

As we point back to the Word, we encourage one another to turn to Scripture to discern what is good. Keeping the Scriptures central in our discipleship relationships helps us teach and train one another to truly live as the women God made us to be—in whatever context He's placed us.

Test yourself and see if you can remember the definition of discipleship from Day Two. If you have trouble, flip back to page 83 and fill in the blanks below.

Discipleship: _____ and _____

in _____ in the context of real _____.

Titus 2:3 says older women are to teach what is _____.

In a room full of Christian women, you'll probably hear the phrase *that's so good* a few times. We nod our heads in agreement with one another—*that's so good*. But is it, really? How can we really know that what's being said and taught is good? Scripture tells us that God Himself is good (1 Chron. 16:34; Ezra 3:11; Ps. 145:5-7; Mark 10:18). Because God is good, we learn to recognize what is good by holding it up against His Word. If it aligns with God's Word and produces good fruit (Matt. 12:33-35), *then* we know something is truly good.

How does this truth confirm the importance of the Bible in our discipling relationships?

What does Titus 2:4-5 say will happen when we teach one another what is good?

In whatever role God has given us, godly living always begins in the home, whether that home consists of one person, a group of roommates, or a husband and wife. But we'll see through our study of Titus that it extends into the culture as well. So, whether you're single, married, a woman living out her faith in the workplace or living this out primarily at home, the message of Titus 2:3-5 is for you! From the oldest to the youngest, the smartest to the simplest, the greatest to the least significant, the truth applies. We have much to learn from one another as we grow in our knowledge of God through His Word together.

One more specific, cultural situation Paul speaks to in this passage involves the relationship between slaves and their masters. As we mentioned earlier, Paul's intent was not to endorse or glorify the practice of slavery in any way. Instead, his instructions offered slaves a sense of dignity and showed they had a valuable role in God's kingdom work.

> **Review Titus 2:9-10.** What did Paul say would be the result of the slaves' right behavior? (Hint: Check out the "so that" phrase in verse 10.)

> What does it mean to "adorn" the gospel? (Compare Titus 2:10 in several different Bible translations to gain a better understanding of the word "adorn." You can use a different Bible or a website like blueletterbible.org or biblegateway.com.)

> How do the instructions given to slaves apply to the modern-day relationship between employers and employees, and how does our behavior in the workplace affect the way we "adorn the gospel"?

The slave/master relationship mentioned here is not a 1:1 comparison to our modern workplace relationships. However, there are principles concerning how we respect and relate to our employers and coworkers that do. To "adorn the gospel" means to make it attractive. Our character, words, and behavior can enhance or damage our gospel witness. That's true at church, at home, and even in the workplace.

> How does our passage for this week teach all Christians to adorn the gospel of grace?

We need men and women who are devoted to teaching and training one another in godliness by studying, knowing, and loving the Scriptures. In His kindness, God has given us everything we need—His Spirit, His Word and one another, our community of faith—to help us become who He made us to be. That's exactly what we're going to talk about as we continue our study tomorrow.

DAY FIVE

Application *(Who Am I to Become?)*

READ TITUS 2:1-10.

Paul's letter to Titus shows us what it looks like to invest in the spiritual growth of a young believer. Likewise, Titus following Paul's instructions shows us the value of humbly submitting to mature Christian leadership. This week's passage, Titus 2:1-10, offers rich instruction for our discipleship relationships within the church. Part of God's good plan for His people is for us to invest in younger believers, as well as follow those who have walked with Jesus longer than we have.

> Do you have a more mature Christian investing in your walk with the Lord? If so, who is she and how has God used her to spiritually encourage you or challenge you to live like Christ?

> Are you investing in the same way in a younger sister in the faith? If so, who is she, and how can you encourage her today?

> If you don't have these women in your life, who are some older and younger women in your church that might could fill these roles? What are some ways you can build relationships with them?

In our twenty-first century church context, it's often not easy to do "life together." Life groups, community groups, or Sunday School classes often segment us by life seasons, which can make it hard to create intergenerational overlap. The one place that does pull us together is corporate worship, but the time is limited, and we have to be intentional to cross age and interest lines in that setting. Many of us lead busy lives with demanding schedules that allow little room for welcoming others to follow us as we follow Jesus. But as we've seen in Titus 2:1-10, we have a biblical responsibility to teach and train one another in godliness. If we fail to fulfill this responsibility, we'll be like little children, tossed to and fro by every wind and wave of teaching. Instead, we need to come alongside one another and build each other up, striving for unity in the faith in the knowledge of God's Son. And we must grow into maturity *together*—with Christ as our ultimate standard (Eph. 4:12-14).

Write a prayer asking God to give you eyes to see those you might be able to learn from or invest in from your local church.

Do you have rich, discipleship relationships? If we asked you to draw a spiritual family tree, would it be easy, or difficult? Fear keeps many of us from engaging in discipleship. We're afraid of asking for help, or afraid of not having the ability to help. Sisters, remember, we have everything we need to teach and train one another in godliness *right now*! With the help of the Holy Spirit, we can go to Scripture, discern its truths, and seek to live them out in community. Though the process of discipleship might be intimidating, it isn't brain surgery. In fact, it's a joy! Consider asking one woman to meet and discuss what you've learned through your study of God's Word this week. You can go over the answers to this study, discuss your church's sermon this week, work on Scripture memory, or read a passage out loud together and talk about it. By God's grace, you can do this, and as you do, you will encourage one another to look more and more like Jesus.

Read the following list of characteristics Paul prescribed to older and younger women. Circle the one(s) you struggle with most.

Reverent	Self-Controlled
Kind	Not slanderers
Pure	Submissive to their husbands
Not slaves to drinking	Hard workers at home

If you circled the whole list, we promise you're not alone. Although Paul's instructions to older and younger women are not comprehensive, they offer a glimpse of the godly living the gospel produces. You may have noticed that the call for "self-control" was directed to each group Paul referenced in 2:1-10 (if not explicitly, then conceptually), meaning people of both genders in all seasons struggle with this issue.

Is self-control something you struggle with, too? If so, how?

Read Galatians 5:17 and write a definition for self-control that you think Paul would agree with.

Empowered by the Holy Spirit, self-control enables Christians to say "yes" to the Spirit while saying "no" to the desires of the flesh. For the older women on Crete, this meant spending their time teaching and training the younger women. For the younger women, it meant practicing self-control among the people who often created the most friction—their husbands and children. But the reality is, we all struggle with self-control. All of us need the Spirit's help to deny our flesh and walk in righteousness.

What is one specific way you can seek to grow in self-control this week?

In what other ways is this week's passage calling you to change the way you live?

As Christians, our relationships with one another should be different from the world around us. Our behavior should be different. Our speech should be different. Our teaching should be different. Our families should be different. Our work should be different. Our very lives should be different! These stark differences should make the gospel even more beautiful to those around us and hopefully cause them to ask, "Why are you so different?"

We'll examine what makes us different in our study next week.

Singing the Gospel

"He Leadeth Me" by Candi Pearson Shelton

Session Five
VIEWER GUIDE

WATCH the Session Five video teaching and take notes in the space below.

DISCUSSION QUESTIONS

1. What part of Courtney and Hunter's conversation resonated with you the most? Why?

2. If a new believer asked you what discipleship is and why she should be involved in it, what would you say?

3. *Discipleship can happen formally and informally.* What does that mean, and how have you seen both take place?

4. Who are some older-in-the-faith believers that have poured into your life? What was their impact on you?

5. Currently, how is discipleship taking place in your life? Who is helping you grow in the faith? Who are you helping to grow in the faith? Why is it important that both of these things are happening?

6. What are the evidences that you are maturing in your faith?

7. What are some of your biggest obstacles to growing in your faith?

8. How does discipleship involve both words and actions?

9. How does this passage call you to display the gospel of grace?

To access the video teaching sessions, use the instructions in the back of your Bible study book.

06

Session Six

Believing the Gospel

Titus 2:11-15

> ¹¹ For the grace of God has appeared, bringing salvation for all people, ¹² instructing us to deny godlessness and worldly lusts and to live in a sensible, righteous, and godly way in the present age, ¹³ while we wait for the blessed hope, the appearing of the glory of our great God and Savior, Jesus Christ. ¹⁴ He gave himself for us to redeem us from all lawlessness and to cleanse for himself a people for his own possession, eager to do good works. ¹⁵ Proclaim these things; encourage and rebuke with all authority. Let no one disregard you.

As I (Courtney) write today, my husband is outside preparing to pour the foundation for a small workshop we're building. Craig is a master builder—as well as a recovering perfectionist—which means that this foundation will be poured with the greatest attention to detail. Why? Because he knows the integrity of the structure will be determined by the integrity of the foundation, not the other way around.

In our passage this week, Paul laid the foundation for our faith and lives. As mentioned in the last session, we don't do good works in order to be saved; we do them as a result of our salvation. We don't pursue godliness to make ourselves acceptable to God; we pursue godliness because God has already declared us acceptable through Jesus. The order is of utmost importance!

MEMORY VERSE

He poured out his Spirit on us abundantly through Jesus Christ our Savior.

TITUS 3:6

MEMORY VERSE HELP FOR THIS WEEK

Read Titus 3:6 aloud five times. Then, try to fill in the blanks for Titus 3:6 below (without looking at the verse). If you don't get it right the first time, keep working at it until you do!

"He _____ out his Spirit on us _____ through Jesus Christ our _____."

If this method works well for you, try downloading The Bible Memory App or the Versify App, which utilize fill-in-the-blank methods to help you commit Scripture to memory. For a different method to memorize Scripture, check out **dwelldifferently.com**.

PRAYER
for the week

Father, thank You for laying a strong foundation for me in the gospel. Thank You for doing everything necessary for my salvation before I did anything. And thank You for giving me the solid truth of Your Word upon which I can stand. Make me a woman who is firmly planted in its truths so that I might weather every storm by Your grace. I pray this in the name of Jesus, who is my firm foundation. Amen.

DAY ONE

Observation *(What Does It Say?)*

READ TITUS 2:11-15.

This passage contains so much for us to know, believe, and live! It's full of deep theological truths, as well as practical implications for life. Hopefully it stirs in you a desire to better understand the gospel and to live more faithfully in light of it. It certainly does for us!

> Write down the first word in verse 11. What do you think Paul was referring to?

"For" is a transition word that ties two sections together. In this case, Paul used it to show exactly what we've been talking about—that our present actions are always anchored in the ancient truth of the gospel. Instead of explaining the gospel, then showing our proper response (in which case he might have used the word "therefore"), Paul flipped it. He told us how we are to live (vv. 1–10), then gave us the reason or basis for our behavior (vv. 11–15)—live this way, *for* (or because) the grace of God has appeared.

> There are several groups of two in this passage. Review the passage and answer the following:
>
> What two things are appearing? Which has already appeared, and which is yet to appear?
>
> What two things is the grace of God instructing us to do?
>
> For what two purposes did Jesus give Himself (v. 14)?

SESSION SIX: BELIEVING THE GOSPEL

What was Titus to do with all authority (v. 15)?

Like the animals that marched two-by-two into the ark in the story of Noah, these groups of two march by us and proclaim the beauty of God's salvation—grace and glory; holiness and good deeds; redemption and sanctification; encouragement and correction. How great and good is our God!

What word is used to describe the attitude in which we are to do good works (2:14)?

What other phrases in this passage could be preceded with that word?

We are not to serve God and do good works in dreaded duty, but with loving eagerness. Eagerness should be a prevailing characteristic of our lives as we embrace holiness and walk in godliness.

Compare our memory passage with this week's passage. What overlap and similarities do you see between them?

	Titus 2:11-13	Titus 3:3-7
What appeared?		
What is our hope?		
What is the result of our salvation?		
What differences do you see?		

Both of these passages summarize the gospel. We hope you're making progress on memorizing Titus 3:3-7. Hiding these words in your heart will not only help you cling to the gospel of grace, but enable you to explain salvation to others more clearly!

DAY TWO

Interpretation *(What Does It Mean?)*

READ TITUS 2:11-15.

We hope you enjoyed reflecting on the grace of God that is found in Jesus! As we consider what this passage means, there are key phrases we need to be careful not to just skim over, or worse, ascribe to them a wrong meaning. So, today, let's slow down and look more closely at those phrases in hopes of truly understanding them.

Paul began with the phrase "the grace of God." As we noted yesterday, he said a few things about that grace: it has appeared, it brought salvation, and it instructs God's people. *To appear* means it was made visible—people were able to see it.

> How did God's grace become visible?

> How does your answer help us understand how grace brought salvation and instructs God's people?

Over two thousand years ago, grace was ultimately made known in Jesus. Paul was able to say that God's grace appeared because the Son of God put on flesh and walked around in this world. God's grace was able to be seen with human eyes.

We noted yesterday that grace has already appeared (through the life, death, and resurrection of Jesus) and that God's glory is going to appear in the future when Christ returns (v. 13).

> When you think about your salvation, do you see that as a past event or something still to take place? Explain.

You might think of salvation as a past event, perhaps remembering the day you were saved. Or maybe your salvation is something in the future—one day you will be saved and go to heaven. But, as we discussed in Session Two, salvation was accomplished in the past, is applied today, and will be realized in the future. Salvation is both for this life and the life to come!

> How might these truths help you wait securely and expectantly "for the blessed hope, the appearing of the glory of our great God and Savior, Jesus Christ"?

> Scripture clearly claims that Jesus is God, that He alone is the Savior of the world, and that He is alive and coming again. Where do you see each of those truths in this passage?

There is a phrase in verse 11 that can be greatly misunderstood and lead to a false doctrine: "all people." As in, grace brings salvation to all people. This could lead to someone embracing the false doctrine of universalism—the belief that everyone will be saved, regardless of their faith (or lack of) in Jesus. On the surface this belief might sound reasonable, but it's not what the Bible teaches and it actually minimizes the death of Christ.

On the night before He was crucified, Jesus cried out in agony, "Father, if you are willing, take this cup away from me—nevertheless, not my will, but yours, be done" (Luke 22:42). In essence, Jesus asked the Father, *if there is any other way for people to be saved, choose that way. Please don't ask me to die.* But Jesus already knew the answer because He told His disciples, "I am the way, the truth, and the life. No one comes to the Father except through me" (John 14:6).

If universalism is true, the death of Jesus was unnecessary, and His Father asked Him to die a pointless death. But universalism is not true, Jesus did die, and, as a result, it's possible for all to be saved. Any person, regardless of background, social status, nationality, or language can come to Jesus and experience salvation. All are invited, but only those who believe will be saved.

Write down any questions you may have about this truth and discuss them with your small group or pastor.

In your own words, write down how Jesus's death on the cross displays the grace of God to all people.

In light of Jesus's willing sacrifice, how do you better understand the phrase "He gave himself" in verse 14?

We mentioned earlier that when Jesus took on flesh the grace of God appeared in human form. And as Jesus left the world, so He will come back (Acts 1:11). Everyone who belongs to Him through faith waits with great hope because the salvation accomplished in His first appearance will be complete when He appears again.

But remember, we aren't to wait passively; we're to wait actively. We're meant to deny godlessness, pursue godliness, and do good works. And may the reality that "there is salvation in no one else, for there is no other name under heaven given to people by which we must be saved" (Acts 4:12) compel us to walk in these ways as we share the great news of this glorious grace with all those around us.

DAY THREE

Interpretation *(What Do Other Scriptures Say?)*

READ TITUS 2:11-15.

This is one of our favorite days of study each week. A core belief orthodox Christians have held throughout the ages is that Scripture interprets Scripture. We embrace that thought and love seeing how the whole counsel of God's Word holds together.

Read Psalm 130:5-7 and answer the following questions:

- What was the psalmist doing?

- How was he able to wait on God?

- What did he want all of God's people (Israel) to do and why?

> **FOR FURTHER READING**
> *From Garden to Glory* by Courtney Doctor

Waiting is always hard. As children, we have to wait for recess, for a snack, or for someone to come and help us. As adults, the waiting can be harder. We wait for test results, an apology, a spouse, a child, a job, or a house. We know what it is to wait.

But not all waiting is the same. *How* we wait matters to God. Do we fret? Are we agitated, angry, anxious? Or do we wait deeply anchored in the goodness and faithfulness of God?

Read the following verses in the Christian Standard Bible (CSB) and fill in the blanks, paying attention to what you learn about how to wait. (You can read Scripture in multiple translations on biblegateway.com or biblehub.com.)

Romans 8:25: Now if we hope for what we do not see, we _____ wait for it with_____.

2 Peter 3:14: Therefore, dear friends, while you wait for these things, make every effort to be found _____ in his sight, at _____.

Scripture instructs us to wait eagerly, patiently, with increasing holiness, and at peace. Does that describe how you wait? Most of us do the exact opposite—we wait anxiously, fearfully, and frantically. We fear the "what ifs" in life—what if something bad happens, what if the results aren't what I want, what if I don't get the thing I long for? One of the best pieces of advice I've ever received is this: change your *what ifs* to *even ifs*. *Even if* the thing I fear happens, *even if* I don't get all I desire, *even if* . . . the Lord is still good, He is still on His throne, and He is coming again. The only way we can wait peacefully and joyfully is if we have placed our hope in the right thing. Our hope can't be in getting the thing we want. Our hope has to be grounded in the goodness of God regardless of what comes. Waiting well is intimately connected with hoping well.

Look up the following verses in the CSB and fill in the blanks, paying attention to where your hope is and how it is described:

2 Corinthians 1:10: He has delivered us from such a terrible death, and he will deliver us. We have put our hope _____ _____ that he will deliver us again.

Hebrews 6:19: We have this hope as an _____ ___ ___ _____, firm and secure. It enters the inner sanctuary behind the curtain.

The author of Hebrews wrote that "faith is the reality of what is hoped for, the proof of what is not seen" (Heb. 11:1). Paul told us that our blessed hope, the thing we are waiting for, is the "appearing of our great God and Savior, Jesus Christ" (Titus 2:13). Jesus is our sure hope, the anchor for our soul. But how do we know that this thing we are to place our hope in—the appearing of His glory—will happen? Well, because Jesus gave us his Word!

Read John 14:3. What did Jesus promise?

Read John 1:14. What has already been seen with human eyes?

Grace and glory have already appeared. Jesus has already come, and "this same Jesus, who has been taken from you into heaven, will come in the same way that you have seen him going into heaven" (Acts 1:11). Friends, he is coming back. It is a sure thing. We can wait patiently, eagerly, and peacefully because the hope of Christ's return is anchored securely in Him—the one who loves us, came to us, died for us, and promised He would come again. Our hope is secure.

Take a moment and practice reciting this week's memory verse.

DAY FOUR

Application *(What Am I to Believe?)*

READ TITUS 2:11-15.

Want to know something about me (Courtney) that might surprise you? I don't like those signs that say "Believe." You know the ones; they're everywhere at Christmas time. And if you have one and decorate with it, sorry! I don't like them because they're so nebulous—*believe what?* Santa, Christmas magic, Jesus, or just the beauty of the season?

Christians are often referred to as "believers." But what we believe is not nebulous, it's concrete. It's real. And our passage for this session is chock full of truths we are to believe!

Let's talk about two types of words that help us understand and interpret Scripture: indicatives and imperatives. Here's how I like to explain them: Indicatives are things that are true; imperatives tell us what to do.

INDICATIVE
A true statement

Scripture contains both, but it's always important to notice the order in which they are used. Indicatives are almost always the basis for imperatives—God tells us something true about Himself or us (indicative) and then tells us how to respond (imperative).

IMPERATIVE
A command or order

This is the order of the gospel. God never tells us to do, become, or obey something so that we will be saved, loved, adopted, or secure. Instead, He tells us to do, become, or obey something because we are already saved, loved, adopted, and secure. The whole book of Ephesians is an example of this. In chapters 1–3, Paul told us what God has done for us and who we are in Him—indicatives. Then, in chapters 4–6, he told us how to live out those truths.

> **Read the following statements from Ephesians and indicate whether they are indicatives or imperatives.**
>
> *In him we have redemption through his blood, the forgiveness of our trespasses, according to the riches of his grace (Eph. 1:7).*
>
> INDICATIVE   IMPERATIVE
>
> *And be kind and compassionate to one another, forgiving one another, just as God also forgave you in Christ (Eph. 4:32).*
>
> INDICATIVE   IMPERATIVE

SESSION SIX: BELIEVING THE GOSPEL

As we focus today on what we are to believe, remember that indicatives always fuel imperatives and not the other way around.

Review Titus 2:11-15. List four to five indicatives you are to believe and four to five imperatives you are to do as a result. (We've provided an example for each list.)

Indicatives you are to believe:

    The grace of God has appeared

Imperatives you are to do:

    Deny godlessness

We're going to focus on the indicatives today and the imperatives tomorrow. We saw on Day One of this week that Scripture clearly claims Jesus is God, that He alone is the Savior of the world, and that He is alive and coming again. Not to belabor the point, but the Christian faith is not a smorgasbord of possible beliefs we get to pick and choose from. We are called to believe everything God says. The following exercise is meant to make us all stop and think about what God is saying in our passage.

(Circle) *yes or no* to indicate whether or not you believe the following statements:

Salvation is by grace alone.	Yes / No
Salvation is available for every person.	Yes / No
Jesus is God.	Yes / No
Salvation is available only through Jesus.	Yes / No
Jesus is coming back.	Yes / No
After we are saved, we are to pursue godliness.	Yes / No
After we are saved, we are to pursue good works.	Yes / No

Hunter and I wish we were sitting across a table from you talking about what you circled for each statement. We're hoping you circled *Yes* on all of them; but if not, we'd also love to discuss any statement in which you circled *No*. It's okay to have doubts or questions. Even one of Jesus's disciples, Thomas, had his fair share. Jesus didn't condemn Thomas, but met him in his doubts. Jesus knows that, for some, faith can be hard and doubt can be easy. And, just as God doesn't pull away from us in our questions, fears, and doubts, He doesn't want us to pull away from Him either. Instead, like Thomas, we should run to God and wrestle through our doubts and questions *with* Him through prayer, His Word, and His people.

If you're currently struggling with doubts or questions, bring those to God in prayer. He is not offended by your honest searching. And pour over His Word, asking Him to reveal truth to you. Have an open heart to hear His response. Process your struggle with a godly friend who can provide insight and perspective to your search.

In the chart below, list your current doubts or questions in the first column below. In the second column, write the name of someone you could talk with about your struggle (this might be the same person you thought of in the last session regarding discipleship). In the last column, put a check in the box after you have met with that person.

My doubts or questions	Who can I talk with?	I have met with them

SESSION SIX: BELIEVING THE GOSPEL

If you're currently not dealing with doubts or questions, write a prayer thanking God for the faith He has given you. Then, if you have family or friends who are currently struggling with their faith, write their names or initials and pray their faith would be restored.

Prayer:

Person I'm praying for:

I once heard someone pray this simple prayer and have incorporated it into my praying for people in my sphere of relationships who are spiritually struggling: "Father, please make faith easy for _____." It is a beautiful prayer and a beautiful thing to desire. The reality is that faith is not easy for everyone. Maybe that includes you. If believing all God has said comes with challenges, doubts, questions, and fears, don't hesitate to take those to God in prayer. Ask Him to meet you in your doubt. Ask him for more insight, understanding, and faith. Ask Him for grace to believe.

DAY FIVE

Application *(Who Am I to Become?)*

READ TITUS 2:11-15.

On day three we read, "Therefore, dear friends, while you wait for these things, make every effort to be found without spot or blemish in his sight, at peace" (2 Pet. 3:14).

Make every effort.

Without spot or blemish.

In Titus 2, Paul wrote that the grace of God is "instructing us to deny godlessness and worldly lusts and to live in a sensible, righteous, and godly way" (2:12). Two verses later he wrote that Jesus gave himself to "redeem us from lawlessness and to cleanse" us for himself (2:14). These two verses from Titus 2 and the verse from 2 Peter 3 are gloriously related.

> In the space provided, write what you think each of these words or phrases mean.
>
> - Make every effort to be found without spot or blemish
>
> - Deny godlessness and worldly lusts
>
> - Live in a sensible, righteous, and godly way
>
> - Redeemed from lawlessness
>
> - Cleansed
>
> (Circle) the actions listed above that God accomplished and <u>underline</u> the actions we are to take.

SESSION SIX: BELIEVING THE GOSPEL

Jesus alone accomplished salvation. It's all His work and we do nothing but receive it. I've heard it said that the only thing we add to our salvation is the sin that necessitated it! But once we come to him in faith and repentance, then He calls us to participate in our sanctification (definition on page 71). We are to make every effort to live in godliness. In other words, once we know Jesus, we should increasingly look like Him, and we participate in that transformation.

Read Ezekiel 36:24-28 and answer the following questions:

- From where was God going to gather the people?

  - Where do we see something similar in our passage this week?

- In verse 25, what did God say He was going to do?

  - Where do we see something similar in our passage this week?

- In verse 27, what did God say He would do and what will the result be?

  - Where do we see something similar in our passage this week? (This one might not be as evident as the first two.)

The verses we just read in Ezekiel 36 were written almost six hundred years before Jesus came to earth. In them, God was promising the new covenant and what it would accomplish. He promised to cleanse us from all unrighteousness, give us new hearts, and make us able to obey His good Word. And we know Jesus has done all of this! Being united to Christ by faith means we have received His perfect righteousness (Rom. 3:21–22), have been cleansed from our unrighteousness (1 John. 1:9), and are now able to pursue righteousness.

D. A. Carson famously said that this pursuit is possible only through "grace-driven effort."[1] We are unable to pursue righteousness without the grace of God *and* we have to put effort into that pursuit by living in obedience.

On Day One we saw that the grace of God has already appeared, bringing us salvation and instructing us to deny godlessness. Meaning, it's grace that makes the pursuit of godliness possible, and grace shows us that godliness and good works are necessary for our sanctification. This is the foundation we talked about in the introduction to this session.

> **Write down everything Titus 2:11-15 tells us to do in response to God's grace. Circle the ones you might need to put a little more grace-driven effort into.**

If you look at the list above, you should see some works that are internal and some that are external. Some are things we are to be (*sensible, righteous, godly*) and some are things we are to do (*deny godlessness and worldly lusts*). From Titus 2 and other New Testament passages, we understand we are to bear internal fruit—love, joy, peace, patience, kindness, goodness, faithfulness, gentleness, and self-control—as well as external fruit—we teach, admonish, disciple, show mercy, help, and serve. Both are part of our pursuit of godliness. Both are the good works we are eager to do. And all of it will require grace-driven effort.

SESSION SIX: BELIEVING THE GOSPEL

This is what the life of a Jesus follower looks like. We press into the grace of God, ask for it, rely on it. Then through it, we work to become all that God desires us to be—holy, fruitful, righteous, sensible, patient, full of good works—slowly, increasingly, and gloriously.

Let's end today by considering what these verses teach us about what we should be doing and who we should be becoming.

> Next to each phrase below, write one concrete example of how you've experienced or are experiencing this in your life. If it's not true of you (yet!), ask God to make it true of you—to give you the grace to strive towards living this way.
>
> I am, more and more,
>
> > denying godlessness:
> >
> > denying worldly lusts:
> >
> > living in ways that are sensible, righteous, and godly:
> >
> > eager to do good works:
> >
> > proclaiming the gospel to others:
> >
> > encouraging and rebuking others through the gospel:

Remember, today's passage is the reason or the basis for the commands Paul gave in the passage we studied last week. That means we could add to the list above things like: teach what is good, be self-controlled, know and proclaim sound doctrine, don't slander or drink too much wine, don't be argumentative . . . (feel free to circle any of these, too!).

Oh friend, we know this is hard work! And sometimes the difficulty comes because the process reveals ways we don't believe or live out the reality of the gospel. If this exercise has been discouraging to you, be encouraged by remembering that it's God's grace that instructs us in these things. As you work on your memory verse, ask God to begin (or continue) a good work in you. Thank Him for pouring out His Spirit on you abundantly. And as you ask Him for the grace needed to believe, do, and become all He desires, praise Him that His grace is abundant and free.

Singing the Gospel

"Christ Our Hope in Life and Death"
by Keith and Kristyn Getty

Session Six
VIEWER GUIDE

WATCH the Session Six video teaching and take notes in the space below.

DISCUSSION QUESTIONS

1. What part of Courtney and Hunter's conversation resonated with you the most? Why?

2. What is your definition of grace?

3. How did grace first appear in your life? How do you experience the grace of God in your daily life?

4. How would you define godliness and how is godliness displayed in your life?

5. How does godlessness rear its ugly head in your life? What is your biggest struggle in living a godly life?

6. How is the power and work of the Holy Spirit essential to you living a godly life?

7. We are living in between the first and second coming of Christ. Would you say you are waiting well for His return? Explain.

8. What does it mean to turn your *what ifs* into *even ifs*? How does remembering the character and promises of God help you do this?

9. How can we help one another wait well and face the future with hope?

10. How does this passage call you to display the gospel of grace?

To access the video teaching sessions, use the instructions in the back of your Bible study book.

07

Session Seven

Insisting on the Gospel

Titus 3:1-8

> ¹ Remind them to submit to rulers and authorities, to obey, to be ready for every good work, ² to slander no one, to avoid fighting, and to be kind, always showing gentleness to all people. ³ For we too were once foolish, disobedient, deceived, enslaved by various passions and pleasures, living in malice and envy, hateful, detesting one another. ⁴ But when the kindness of God our Savior and his love for mankind appeared, ⁵ he saved us—not by works of righteousness that we had done, but according to his mercy— through the washing of regeneration and renewal by the Holy Spirit. ⁶ He poured out his Spirit on us abundantly through Jesus Christ our Savior ⁷ so that, having been justified by his grace, we may become heirs with the hope of eternal life. ⁸ This saying is trustworthy. I want you to insist on these things, so that those who have believed God might be careful to devote themselves to good works. These are good and profitable for everyone.

When was the last time you received good news? Maybe you asked the server for your check at the restaurant and he told you someone had already paid for your meal. That's good news! Or maybe your supervisor informed you that you were up for a promotion. Also good news! Maybe you received favorable test results from the doctor after a major health scare. You probably put that in the category of really good news!

What was your response when you received such good news? If you're like us, you told someone (or lots of someone's) about it! This week, we're going to see how the gospel is such good news we can't help but proclaim it to the world around us.

We want to point out a slight change to the first two days of personal study. Unlike in previous weeks, we'll consider *What Does It Say?* and *What Does It Mean?* on both study days. On Day One we'll discuss how we're to be different from the world around us, and on Day Two we'll dive into why we're different. We think this approach will help us believe and embrace the truth of this beautiful gospel passage in a way that encourages us to more genuinely live it out.

MEMORY VERSE

> . . . so that, having been justified by His grace, we may become heirs, with the hope of eternal life.

TITUS 3:7

MEMORY VERSE HELP FOR THIS WEEK

Can you believe it? You've made it to the final portion of our Scripture memory for this study! This week, we're finishing up our gospel-packed section with Titus 3:7, which says we are heirs with the hope of eternal life. As you work on this short portion of the verse, turn it into a prayer. It could look something like this, "Lord, thank you for making me righteous through Your Son, Jesus, and for granting me the hope of eternal life in Him." Then, be sure to review the whole memory passage. This will help you regularly use it to remember the life changing truth of the gospel.

PRAYER
for the week

Father, I confess it's challenging to do good to all people, especially those who are difficult to be around. Help me to remember the kindness You extend to me in Christ, and prompt me to show kindness to others—just as You've done for me. Thank You for the good work You began in me when You opened my heart to the good news of the gospel. Help me live in a way that reflects the inward reality of what you have done in me through Your Son, Jesus. I pray these things in His name. Amen.

DAY ONE

Observation and Interpretation

(What Does It Say? What Does It Mean?)

READ TITUS 3:1-8.

Paul's letter to Titus was likely written toward the end of the apostle Paul's life. Think about that for a minute. If you were nearing the end of your life, what would you want to communicate to your true son or daughter in the faith? In this week's passage, we see that Paul insisted on the good news of the gospel, knowing the importance of the connection between right belief and right behavior. This short but potent section is like his gospel manifesto.

> Before we dig into this section, it's helpful to remember where we've been. What did we learn from Titus 2:12-15 about the effect of God's grace in our lives?

Last week, we saw that God's grace should compel Christians to godly behavior and good works as we await Christ's return. In our passage this week, Paul told Titus to encourage the gospel-driven community on Crete to display their hope in Christ as they engaged the world around them. This is the same good work you and I are called to today.

> In the first two verses of chapter three, Paul encouraged Titus to remind Cretan believers to do seven things. List them here:
>
> Verse 1
>
> -
> -
> -

Verse 2

-
-
-
-

Previously, we learned that Cretans were known for being liars, detestable, and greedy (Titus 1:12). How did Paul's instructions to believers in Titus 3:1-2 contrast the behavior of the culture around them?

Cretans who had been made alive in Christ were supposed to look different from the people around them—people who were still dead in their trespasses and sins (Eph. 2:1-5). By God's grace, they were to display God's saving work in their world by living in line with the blessing they received in Christ. They were blessed to be a blessing.

Who did Paul instruct the believers to show gentleness toward in verse 2?

Because (as Paul said in Titus 1:12) Cretans were generally known to be liars, evil beasts, and lazy gluttons, it's safe to say selfishness was the general vibe in Crete. It was praiseworthy to be characterized by being boastful and assertive in the Roman world. In contrast, Paul encouraged Cretan Christians to be selfless. The Christian call for humility and deference was strange (and abhorrent) in this cultural context. As Cretan Christians made themselves ready for every good work, one of the most helpful things they could do was to remember who they were before Christ—people who didn't deserve the selfless good work of Christ. No different from the godless people around them.

What did Paul say in Titus 3:3 the Cretan believers were like *before* Christ?

What pronoun did Paul use in Titus 3:3 and why is that significant?

Paul didn't set himself above the Cretans. He was in the same boat they were in before Christ. Remembering the bad news—who they were before God's grace appeared in their lives—set the Cretan believers up to treasure the very good news that Titus 3:4 brings. Paul used the stark contrast between verses three and four to remind them that apart from Christ, they (and all of us!) were no better than the culture around them—foolish, deceived, and utterly hopeless.

BUT, according to verse 5, God _____ them.

At the center of this passage, we find the phrase that changed absolutely everything—*God saved us*. This truth—the truth that God can rescue us from our depravity through his Son, Jesus (Col. 1:13)—has the power to transform not only the lives of the first century church, but also our lives, our communities, and the culture around us.

Tomorrow, we'll think more about these things, but as we close today, take a brief moment to reflect upon the saving grace of God as you review the Scripture memory verse for the week.

DAY TWO

Observation and Interpretation

(What Does It Say? What Does It Mean?)

READ TITUS 3:1-8.

Do you ever find yourself trying to earn God's grace? Do you worry that God doesn't—or can't—love you? Or, do you continually strive to do all the right things so that He will love you?

Despite our endless attempts to save ourselves, we can't do anything to make ourselves right before God. Scripture says that all our righteous acts are filthy rags (Isa. 64:6), which is why we need a Savior. While salvation doesn't come through our good works, good works were required for salvation. Not ours, but Christ's. Today, we'll consider how Christ did the necessary greatest work to reconcile sinners like us to a righteous and holy God. That, friends, is very good news!

> **Read Titus 3:4** and fill in the blank below.
>
> But when the kindness of God our Savior and His love for mankind
> _____.

It's always a blessing to reflect upon the greatest news we have ever received—"today in the city of David, a Savior was born for you, who is the Messiah, the Lord" (Luke 2:11). Centuries ago, the kindness of God appeared when a humble baby boy was born to a virgin in a lowly stable. All the promises God made throughout the Old Testament were fulfilled in a person who could be touched, hugged, and eventually, pierced for our transgressions. The climax of God's love for us was on full display when He sent his Son.

> What life-changing verb in verse 5 describes what happened as a result of His coming?

All three members of the Trinity were involved in the work of salvation. **Review verses 4-7,** and list the work of each one:

- God:

- The Holy Spirit:

- Jesus:

> **FOR FURTHER READING**
>
> *Delighting in the Trinity* by Michael Reeves

According to his mercy, God expressed his love and kindness toward sinners by saving us through his Son, Jesus. Jesus took the punishment we rightly deserved. Because of His work on the cross, we are regenerated (born again) and renewed through the Holy Spirit. The Spirit makes us alive in Christ and we become heirs with Him, receiving all the blessings that Christ deserves. As David Garner said: "Salvation is purposed by the Father, accomplished by the Son, and applied by the Holy Spirit."[1] This, friends, is the greatest news of all!

Does Titus 3:1-8 offer any reason why God should save us? Explain.

Like the believers in Crete, before Christ we were foolish, disobedient, and deceived. Praise God; He offers us salvation based on His mercy. Jesus died in our place, absorbing the wrath of God against our sin. As a result, we are no longer condemned, but are declared innocent. This is very good news! And the good news doesn't stop here.

Along with freedom from the penalty of sin, what does verse 7 say we receive as a result of the saving work of God?

Jesus died the death we deserved (Rom. 3:23; 6:23), making the way for us to be reconciled to God (Rom. 5:10), so we can become heirs with the hope of eternal life (Titus 3:7). What a gift! But while the gift is freely offered, it is not automatically bestowed. We must respond to this incredibly good news by turning from our sin and trusting in Christ. It is the only right response. If you haven't yet trusted in Christ, run to him, confess you are a sinner, and ask Him to save you. Nothing delights Him more!

If you have trusted Christ for your salvation, close by taking a moment to praise Him for this life changing good news.

DAY THREE

Interpretation *(What Do Other Scriptures Say?)*

READ TITUS 3:1-8.

To communicate clearly, repetition is important. That's definitely the case at my (Hunter's) house. My husband and I are deep in the training phase of parenting. We regularly tell our elementary age kiddos, "Please try again with kindness and respect." We often remind our preschooler, "Let's think of our friends first." And our 18-month-old requires the repeated instruction, "Stop, please." The repetition helps us emphasize our point, create rhythm and structure, and reinforce the message we're trying to get across.

The Bible authors also used repetition. That's why it's important to pay attention to repeated words and phrases in the biblical text to clearly understand the message the writer was trying to communicate.

> What two-word phrase in Titus 3:1 is repeated throughout the book?

> Consider other instances in which we've already seen the phrase *good work(s)* in the book of Titus (1:16; 2:7,14). What does the repetition of this phrase tell us about Paul's message?

The good works we set our hands to don't earn our salvation, but they do express it. Said another way, we've not just been saved *from* something, but we've been saved *for* something. By His grace, our good works are the proper response to our salvation and the proof of the good work He began in our hearts. The gospel works to change not only our hearts but our entire lives. This life change will also impact those around us.

The only way we can engage in these good works is because of the good work God has done in us. This week we've read terms like *salvation*, *regeneration*, *justification*, and *eternal life*—words we often throw around interchangeably without stopping to ponder their meanings.

Look up the following verses and write a short definition of each term:

- Salvation (Rom. 5:9):

- Regeneration (Ezek. 36:25-27):

- Justification (Rom. 5:18):

- Eternal Life (John 17:3):

Because of Jesus, we can be rescued from the wrath of God's judgment, made alive, declared righteous, and given the opportunity to know God forever! The more we understand the life-changing impact and origin of this good news, the more we will live in light of it and share it with others.

Recently, I had a friend (who is a new follower of Christ) ask what she should say when asked to share her testimony. She was a little unsure because that word—*testimony*—can carry a level of intimidation and pressure. However, to share a testimony simply means to give evidence to God's saving work in your life.

Some of you can probably rattle off your testimony in ninety seconds, closing with a direct invitation to follow Jesus. Some of you may be a little less sure how to communicate how God has worked in your life. Others might not know the saving power of the gospel in a personal way, so you really don't have a testimony. If you fall into the latter category, know that it's by God's grace you are considering these truths today. We want to encourage you to find a friend, mentor, or pastor who can help you discuss any questions you have about what it means to follow Jesus. Whether you're a seasoned follower of Christ, a new believer, or you're simply exploring Christianity, we're praying that the saving power of God through the gospel will leave you in awe of God's grace today.

Use the prompts below to help you work through the basics of your testimony. This will help you be ready to share the hope you have in Jesus (1 Pet. 3:15). Pray for opportunities to tell others about the good work God has done in your heart. If you don't yet know Jesus as your personal Savior, answer the questions in parenthesis.

Before you knew Jesus, what did your life revolve around? Where did you look for security, peace, and happiness? (Where do you currently look for security, peace, and happiness?)

When did you hear and understand the good news of the gospel? What was your response to Jesus Christ? What changed in your life when you began following Christ? (What keeps you from responding to Jesus in faith and following Him?)

Now that you know Jesus, where do you find your security and hope? How do you currently see God working in your life? How do you live life differently than before you came to know Jesus? (If you're interested in following Jesus or want more information about that decision, who can you reach out to and what questions do you have?)

Remember that the great saving work God has done and continues to do in our hearts motivates us to good works and engaging in the lives of those around us. As we close our study today, continue to reflect on the good news of the gospel by reviewing your memory verses. This passage will help you continually rehearse the gospel by reminding you who you were before Christ, what God has done for you in Christ, and who you are because of Christ.

Take a moment and practice reciting this week's memory verse.

DAY FOUR

Application *(What Am I to Believe?)*

READ TITUS 3:1-8.

A few weeks ago, my (Hunter's) in-laws brought a few boxes of my husband's old belongings to our house. They had cleaned out their attic and felt it was time for him to assume responsibility for the trophies, yearbooks, collages, and metals he had accumulated over the years. As he and I went through the boxes, we were in awe of how much he has changed. By God's good grace, he is not the same person he was back then.

In similar fashion, Paul encouraged us to do the same in Titus 3:1-8—to remember who we were so we can marvel at what God has done.

> How does remembering who we were help us be more aware of our need for God's grace (vv. 3-5)?

Review Paul's list in verse 3. Considering your life before Christ, write how you would describe your old life in the column on the left. Then, review verses 4-7 and describe Christ's work in you and who you are in Him in the column on the right.

Who I Was Before Christ	Who I Am in Christ
For I too was once . . .	But when the kindness of God our Savior and His love for mankind appeared, He . . .

SESSION SEVEN: INSISTING ON THE GOSPEL

Check the boxes that are true:

☐ God saved me according to my works

☐ God saved me because my good works outweigh my bad works

☐ God saved me because of His mercy

We often live as though God saved us because our good works outweigh our bad, but Titus 3:4-7 reveals that God saved us according to His mercy. This is marvelous news for sinners like us!

Look up the word *mercy* in the dictionary and write a definition you think Paul would agree with:

How does knowing we contribute nothing to our salvation offer you hope for your sibling, aunt, cousin, parent, friend, or coworker you've been praying will come to faith in Christ?

Because of God's mercy, even though we were dead in our sin, we have been made alive with Christ (Eph. 2:4-5). God does not save us because of our goodness, track record, potential, or influence. He saves us because of His kindness and mercy, which He richly poured out on us through Jesus Christ. Paul says that this saying—this gospel news—is trustworthy (Titus 3:8), which means we can rely on it.

Why did Paul want Titus to insist on these things (the truths of the gospel found throughout the letter but specifically in this passage)?

Right belief leads to good works. Titus was to insist on the gospel so the Cretans would make it of first importance in their lives. He was to insist on their insistence of it. Only with that focus would they be equipped to do good works. What do you find yourself being insistent upon? Is it a certain approach to nutrition, schooling option, niche doctrinal issue, political party, or clothing brand? If someone were to look at your posts on social media, your text messages, or to overhear your conversations, what would they say you're all about? As Christians, we are to be known for our insistence on the gospel of God's grace.

List two to three things you find yourself insisting on.

If you're insisting on the wrong things, how will that affect the good works you do? How can you change the focus back to the gospel?

God gave us His Word so that we might know Him and believe the story He's writing! To really know and insist on the gospel, we have to be immersed in God's Word by regularly reading and studying it, by hearing it preached in our local churches, and by preaching it to our own hearts every single day.

What is one way you want to grow in your ability to insist on the gospel in your life?

May we be women who increasingly believe and insist upon the good news of the gospel, so we would be careful to devote ourselves to good works.

Learning our memory verses (Titus 3:3-7) provides the opportunity for us to grow in our knowledge of this gloriously good news as we seek to live it out. Take some time to review those verses now.

DAY FIVE

Application *(Who Am I to Become?)*

READ TITUS 3:1-8.

Have either of these things happened to you?

You cut someone off in traffic only to remember you have your church's bumper sticker stuck on the back of your vehicle.

You are visibly and verbally exasperated in the checkout line only to look down and see you're wearing a Christian T-shirt.

> **FOR FURTHER HELP APPLYING THE GOSPEL**
> *A Gospel Primer for Christians: Learning to See the Glories of God's Love*
> by Milton Vincent

Ugh.

Sadly, we often act in ways that contradict the gospel of grace we profess. Sure, we all have our moments, but those who claim Christ ought to be living, breathing examples of what it looks like to belong to Him. This week's text encourages us to live as representatives of God's grace by preparing ourselves for every good work in the world.

Consider your current season of life and the roles God has given you. What keeps you from being ready for every good work?

Review Titus 3:1-2. How does the kindness of God our Savior (v. 4) inform our understanding of Paul's instructions for how we engage culture? How does kindness describe how you should treat and speak about others, especially those different from you who don't know Christ?

Where would you like to see more consistency in your life between what you believe and how you live? List two to three areas and ask God for His help!

The message of the gospel is not just for the non-believer but also for the Christian—every single day. We must remember the good work that God did in us through His Son in order to rightly engage in the good works He's set before us.

How does remembering the gospel (Titus 3:3-7) motivate us to do good works?

Sometimes, "remembering the gospel" can feel a little cliche. What does it actually mean to remember the gospel? Well, you've been doing that all week! Remembering the gospel is reflecting on who you were before Christ and who you are in him. It means pushing back against the lies of the enemy with the truth of God's Word. It is acknowledging the ways you're falling short and humbly asking for God's help.

When have you recently found yourself needing to remember you aren't saved by your righteous works, but by God's mercy? How could preaching the gospel to yourself have helped in that moment?

Maybe you snapped at your children when they asked the same question for the tenth time. Instead of resolving they deserved it, or wallowing in shame, preach the gospel to yourself by remembering the patience of God to sinners (Rom. 2:4). This presents an opportunity to apologize to your kiddos and welcome them to reflect upon the kindness of God through Christ as you seek to be patient with one another.

You may have failed to live up to the expectations you set for yourself at school, at work, or in other areas of your life. Remind yourself that your work will never be enough. You will always fall short of the glory of God (Rom. 3:23) and can only be made right with Him through what Christ has done for you (2 Cor. 5:21).

You might feel like you deserve more than what you've received because you're working hard for the Lord! But when you preach the gospel to yourself you'll be reminded that you have not received what you deserve (death), but you've been given infinitely more than you deserve through the saving work of Christ (Rom. 6:23).

Instead of brushing such feelings under the rug, seek to apply the gospel to whatever hard thing you're walking through and allow its truths to renew your mind (Rom. 12:2). The more you meditate on the saving grace of God and apply it to your own life, the more you'll be ready to share this gospel hope with the people around you!

What barriers do you face in sharing the gospel with those around you? List two to three things that would help you overcome those barriers.

Who is one person you can share the good news of the gospel with this week?

My (Hunter's) grandmother, Grand Ann, suffered from debilitating memory loss at the end of her life. Though she couldn't remember to take her medication in the morning, and she often forgot people's names, she was always talking about the love of Jesus. Even in her feeble state, the good news of the gospel was constantly on her lips. Why? Because she had a habit of regularly rehearsing its truths.

When you reach the end of your life, what of your spoken words do you want to be known for? Consider the things you constantly meditate on. Are they moving you closer to or further away from the woman in Christ you want to become? May we, like Paul and Grand Ann, spend every moment we have insisting on the good news of the gospel, knowing it is the most important message of all.

Singing the Gospel

"Amazing Grace" by The Worship Initiative

Session Seven
VIEWER GUIDE

WATCH the Session Seven video teaching and take notes in the space below.

DISCUSSION QUESTIONS

1. What part of Courtney and Hunter's conversation resonated with you the most? Why?

2. The passage we're memorizing for our study of Titus is covered in this session. What part of the memory passage stands out to you and why?

3. Share what it was like when you first realized your need for Christ. What was your life like before Christ? How did the Holy Spirit bring you to the point of understanding your need for the Savior?

4. Courtney and Hunter talk about how we should be singing the song of the gospel in our lives. What does that mean to you? Are you singing the song of the gospel on a regular basis? If so, how? If not, what's hindering you?

5. How does the power of the gospel continue to transform you beyond just the moment you were saved?

6. How should your life as a follower of Jesus look different than the lives of those around you who don't know Him? Are you currently giving evidence of that difference? If so, in what ways? If not, why not?

7. What does it mean to rehearse the good news of the gospel? How does doing so shape the way you live your life—the way you face trials, the decisions you make, the way you view your purpose, etc.?

8. What does it mean that you were not saved *by* good works but were saved *for* good works? What are some Spirit-powered, Spirit-led good works you see being exhibited by women in this group? By others in your community of faith?

9. How does this passage call you to display the gospel of grace?

To access the video teaching sessions, use the instructions in the back of your Bible study book.

08

Session Eight

Living the Gospel

Titus 3:9-15

⁹ But avoid foolish debates, genealogies, quarrels, and disputes about the law, because they are unprofitable and worthless. ¹⁰ Reject a divisive person after a first and second warning. ¹¹ For you know that such a person has gone astray and is sinning; he is self-condemned.

¹² When I send Artemas or Tychicus to you, make every effort to come to me in Nicopolis, because I have decided to spend the winter there. ¹³ Diligently help Zenas the lawyer and Apollos on their journey, so that they will lack nothing. ¹⁴ Let our people learn to devote themselves to good works for pressing needs, so that they will not be unfruitful. ¹⁵ All those who are with me send you greetings. Greet those who love us in the faith. Grace be with all of you.

We can't believe this is the last week in our study of Titus. What a joy it's been spending this time together in Paul's short but significant letter to his "true son" in the faith. As we study these last seven verses, we'll see that Paul ended his letter much like he began—instructing Titus to insist on sound doctrine, silence false teachers, live in grace, pursue godliness, and devote oneself to good works. There is much to learn from Paul's focus on the essentials of the faith and the importance of knowing, believing, and displaying the gospel of grace in all things.

MEMORY VERSE

This week we will review all the verses you've memorized. Take a moment to write down the whole passage, then place it somewhere you can see it and reference it often, such as on your bathroom mirror, by your kitchen sink, in the shower (make sure it's in a plastic bag!), or in your vehicle. This passage will help you remember and proclaim the truth of the gospel whenever you can, wherever you go!

> [3] For we too were once foolish, disobedient, deceived, enslaved by various passions and pleasures, living in malice and envy, hateful, detesting one another. [4] But when the kindness of God our Savior and his love for mankind appeared, [5] he saved us—not by works of righteousness that we had done, but according to his mercy—through the washing of regeneration and renewal by the Holy Spirit. [6] He poured out his Spirit on us abundantly through Jesus Christ our Savior [7] so that, having been justified by his grace, we may become heirs with the hope of eternal life.
>
> **TITUS 3:3-7**

PRAYER
for the week

Father, thank You that Your Word is true and has been given to us. I pray You would again show me the depths of Your wisdom and knowledge. Grant me understanding that I might know how to align my life with Your Word and ways—and that godliness would increasingly be evident in me. I pray my life would be devoted to knowing, believing, loving, and displaying the gospel of grace more and more until that glorious day I see You face-to-face. In Jesus's name. Amen.

DAY ONE

Observation *(What Does It Say?)*

READ TITUS 3:9-15.

Do you have one of "those" family members? You know the type—the one who loves to stir things up and cause conflict. The one who loves to play devil's advocate and argue about almost everything? Maybe you've not experienced this personally, but you've seen someone like this impact a friend's family. Regardless of how you know this person, you're clearly aware of the damage a divisive, argumentative, quarrelsome person can cause. Don't you wish someone would lovingly confront the agitator and put a stop to the chaos?

Paul told Titus to be that person—the one who steps in to confront people who are wreaking havoc in the family of God. Paul may have sounded harsh here, but he was again acting like the "mama-bear" we discussed in Session Four. Paul loved God's church and was zealous to not only insist on sound doctrine and sound living but also to silence divisive and disruptive people. Ultimately, it is God Himself who loves His church, insists on sound doctrine, and protects His children.

> **Go back and read Titus 3:8.** Why are the instructions in verse 8 and verse 9 essential to right living? What contrasts do you see?

> Make a list of what Paul said to avoid in verse 9. What reasons did he give for doing so?

> **Read verse 10 in the ESV or NIV.** What three action steps are we to take toward a divisive person?

> What was Paul's reasoning for this action (v. 11)?

SESSION EIGHT: LIVING THE GOSPEL

Paul instructed Titus to avoid divisive conversations and reject divisive people because both the quarrelers and the quarrels are foolish and disruptive to the church.

It's tempting to skip over Paul's closing comments (vv. 12-15) thinking they are no more than a simple goodbye that has no relevance for us. But that would be a mistake. First, remember that "*all* Scripture is inspired by God and is profitable for teaching, for rebuking, for correcting, for training in righteousness" (2 Tim. 3:16, emphasis mine). Which means there is something for us to learn, believe, and apply in these verses. Secondly, the names listed are significant. These verses beautifully highlight God's mission in the world and the importance of our interdependence on one another as we participate together in that mission.

According to verses 12-13:

Who was being sent to Crete?

Who might have been leaving Crete and for what purpose?

Circle where Paul said he was going to be spending the winter (v. 12).

146   TITUS

What was Paul's final wish for the people of Crete and his reason for that desire? How is this similar to what you studied last week?

What was Paul's last sentence in this letter? How does it compare to how he began the letter (1:4)?

The letter to Titus began with grace and ended with grace. In between we've seen the need to pursue godliness and good works—but those are always nestled deeply in the grace of God. We only desire godliness and good works because of God's grace and we can only pursue them by God's grace. So, to close the day, rest in the grace of God as you work on your memory verses, knowing that it is a good work that will bear good fruit.

DAY TWO

Interpretation (What Does It Mean?)

READ TITUS 3:9-15.

As we noted yesterday, these verses sound harsh to our modern ears. Should we really reject people and avoid what they have to say? Our current cultural compulsion is to either "cancel" everyone or do the opposite—accept everyone, their opinions, and the way they choose to live. Let's lean in and learn why Paul would say such a thing.

CHURCH DISCIPLINE

"The act of excluding someone who professes to be a Christian from membership in the church and participation in the Lord's Supper for serious unrepentant sin—sin they refuse to let go of."[1]

Not only do these words sound harsh, they are also challenging because they deal with church discipline. The idea of church discipline might be entirely foreign to you, especially since many churches don't practice it in any form. If so, see the definition in the margin and check out the resources listed.

> How does the church discipline definition reflect what you read in Titus 3:9-11?

FOR FURTHER READING

A Place to Belong
by Megan Hill

What Is a Healthy Church?
by Mark Dever

Notice several things in this definition. First, church discipline applies only to professing believers. Of course, unbelievers have unrepentant sin. They have not yet turned to God in faith. Also, they don't yet have the power of the Holy Spirit dwelling in them or the grace necessary to align their lives with the Word of God.

Second, church discipline is for *unrepentant* sin. The following is what my (Courtney's) pastor says every week as he's offering the Lord's Supper: "So if you have not yet come to faith in Jesus Christ, turning from your sin and trusting him alone for salvation; or if you are under church discipline here or any other church; or if you are *clinging to sin and unwilling to repent*, then rather than coming forward to receive the elements, we would invite you to use this time for prayer and reflection."

148   TITUS

Then he adds, "But for all humble sinners who trust in the Lord Jesus Christ, be assured that your sins and vices, your weaknesses and doubts, should not keep you from this Table. Jesus Christ welcomes all of His people to come and find strength and healing in Him."

I love these words because they remind me, week after week, that it's not sinners who receive church discipline (or else we would all be under it!)—church discipline is for those who are *clinging* to sin and *unwilling* to repent. My vices, sins, doubts, and weaknesses don't keep me from taking the Lord's Supper, but my refusal to repent of them should. In fact, the Lord's Supper strengthens me in my weakness, comforts me in my doubts, and fortifies me as I fight sin in my life.

Let's be honest, when it comes to church discipline, many of us struggle with it. Why?

1. We've seen it done poorly and want nothing more to do with it.

2. We've never seen it practiced, so it sounds foreign, antiquated, and harsh.

3. We struggle with authority, especially church authority, so we totally balk at the idea.

Do any of these scenarios describe you? Write your honest thoughts and questions about the concept of church discipline.

Cyprian, a north African theologian from the third century, famously said, "You can't have God as your Father unless you have the church for your Mother."[2] What he meant was that the church should function in much the same way a caring mother does—she loves, protects, feeds, instructs, and disciplines her children.

In your own words, describe either how the church has been like a mother to you or how it could be.

> How could the instructions in Titus 3:9-11, if practiced well, be profitable and restorative to the divisive ones, as well as the whole church?

Titus had been sent to Crete to finish establishing the church and raise up church leaders. He was to make sure the doctrine being proclaimed was sound so that the hearts of people in the church were protected and they could spiritually grow. These particular instructions to Titus about discipline, though they sound harsh, were not vindictive in any way, but born out of Paul's great love for the church and his desire for it to flourish.

> How does this reminder of Paul's purpose in writing help us better understand these verses?

Let's finish today with a closer look at verse 13.

> What do you think Paul meant when he told Titus to "diligently help Zenas the lawyer and Apollos on their journey, so that they will lack nothing"?

Zenas and Apollos had most likely been on Crete helping Titus. However, it now seems they were preparing to leave and go somewhere else to serve God and proclaim the gospel. Paul wanted the church in Crete to help send them on their way by providing for their physical needs.

This is a picture of how the church should function. God calls His people to be on mission—to go, to give, to serve. Some do more going and some do more giving, but all serve to fulfill God's desire to seek and save the lost.

As you work on your memory verses today, ask God how you can devote yourself to good works and join Him on His great mission.

DAY THREE

Interpretation *(What Do Other Scriptures Say?)*

READ TITUS 3:9-15.

Discipline is a loaded word. We like it as an adjective but not as a verb. Meaning, most of us would love to be described as disciplined—someone with strong follow through, self-control, and dedication to things like exercise, Bible reading, healthy eating, or even cleaning. But few of us want to be disciplined—have someone correct, punish, or regulate our wrong behavior. This use of the word indicates someone or something has authority over us, and that thought doesn't always sit well.

Yesterday we mentioned that some of us struggle with the concept of the church as an authority in our lives. As we wrestle with this thought, let's see how other Scripture passages help us understand the heart of God regarding discipline.

> Read Hebrews 12:5-13 and answer the following questions:
>
> What is the motivation for God's discipline (v. 6)?
>
> What does God's discipline indicate about our relationship with Him (vv. 7-8)?
>
> What is the intended result of the discipline (vv. 11,13)?

This passage beautifully shows the heart of our perfect Father. He disciplines His children out of love so we will live godly, righteous lives and not be "lame . . . but healed." His discipline is for our good and for our growth!

> Read John 15:1-2. What similarities do you see between these verses and the Hebrews 12 passage?

God lovingly disciplines His children to increase fruitfulness. Sometimes, sound churches are called to be the means of this discipline. Remember, only professing believers, walking in willful, unrepentant sin, should be under church discipline. This discipline should also be done in love, for their good, and their restoration.

Read Matthew 18:15-20 and answer the following:

What steps are to be taken to restore a fellow believer?

How does Titus 3:10 reflect this passage? (Note: To regard someone as a "Gentile or tax collector" meant to treat that person as if he or she were an unbeliever.)

Read Romans 16:17-18. Who are we to watch out for and how will we recognize them?

Why are we to avoid them?

Avoiding, rejecting, correcting, and disciplining someone sounds so harsh. But, if that person is a believer walking in habitual sin, then the most loving thing we can do is correct them with a heart to restore. The reality is that divisive, quarrelsome people harm themselves, their listeners, their families, and their churches. The beauty of church discipline is that it is for the good of everyone involved. The divisive person benefits by being rebuked and, Lord willing, restored. The listeners, families, and churches benefits by being protected.

There is one clear lesson in all this: our actions, good or bad, impact those around us. Divisive people harm the church, but godly people strengthen the church! At the end of most of his letters Paul mentions the godly people around him—his coworkers, devoted to good works. These friendships encouraged him and spurred him on to faithful ministry.

This was the case in his letter to Titus. Paul was planning to send either Artemas or Tychicus to Crete. We don't know anything about Artemas but read the passages below to learn more about Tychicus.

How is Tychicus described and what do we learn about him in the following passages?

- Acts 20:1-4

- Ephesians 6:21

- Colossians 4:7

Tychicus was probably the one who carried the letters from Paul to both the Ephesian and Colossian churches. This meant he was also most likely the first to read and explain the letters. He was clearly a trusted ministry partner who brought Paul much joy. I hope you have a Tychicus or two in your life!

In Titus 3:13, Paul also mentioned Zenas and Apollos. Zenas remains a mystery (other than that he was a lawyer), but we know a lot about Apollos.

Read Acts 18:24-28. Describe Apollos and his journey.

Has anyone "taken you aside" to instruct you and help you grow in "the way of God"? If so, who? How did they help you?

Is there anyone in your life you could help like Priscilla and Aquila helped Apollos? If so, who? What actions steps will you take to establish and foster that relationship?

Priscilla and Aquila are examples of the kind of discipleship we've been talking about throughout this study. They saw a younger brother who loved and served the Lord but needed some guidance. They came alongside him and taught him more about God and His Word. They instructed him, prayed for him, encouraged him, and rejoiced in him. Apollos was humble and received their help—I suspect he was deeply grateful for their investment in him. What a beautiful picture of discipleship!

Read 1 Corinthians 3:5-9. Knowing Paul wrote these words, describe how Paul viewed his relationship with Apollos?

These beautiful verses show us the interconnectedness and interdependence needed between God's people. Apollos needed Priscilla and Aquila to instruct him and help him grow in his faith. Paul and Apollos worked side by side, relying on and rejoicing in each other's work. Oh friends, there is much for us to take heed of and live by in these verses!

Tomorrow we'll dig deeper into the idea of joining our lives to God's mission. But to close today, work on your memory verses. Know that your labor will not be in vain—and will not be for you alone. Those around you will benefit from your godliness and good works!

Take a moment and practice reciting this week's memory verse.

DAY FOUR

Observation

(What Am I to Believe? Who Am I to Become?)

READ TITUS 3:9-15.

Heads up! We're changing things around today and tomorrow. Today we will ask both the *What Am I to Believe?* and *Who Am I to Become?* questions. Tomorrow, we will review the whole letter of Titus and discuss all we've seen and learned.

From this letter, it's evident Titus was dealing with some argumentative, divisive people in Crete. But it's hard to imagine the situation in Crete being worse than our current cultural moment. We don't have to look very far to find divisive people and foolish debates. We are surrounded by "cancel culture," tribalism, ghosting, hate crimes, and so much more. We reject people who disagree with us over politics, news channels, educational choices, and other non-essential theological issues. Was Paul commending this kind of action? Are we supposed to "cancel" those we don't agree with or who debate us on these topics? No!

Disagreeing with someone is not wrong. Healthy arguments and debates can be helpful. We don't need to agree on every issue. And we certainly don't need to reject someone just because we don't agree. In fact, we need to do a better job of living in unity with those people. However, we need to be careful not to get involved in foolish conversations or worthless disputes. Paul told Titus not to engage with the false teachers and others in pointless arguments about the law, genealogies, and other things that diverted attention away from the gospel. We need to heed this command also.

What might be a foolish debate or argument we could get wrapped up in but should avoid?

Some might want to passionately argue their view on a tertiary issue as if it was the only correct view. Just because people are passionate about something doesn't mean it's worthy of your time or energy. If it diverts time and energy away from what's most important, proclaiming the truth of the gospel, it's best to just walk away.

How might a person championing foolish and disruptive arguments become divisive?

The divisive people Paul instructed Titus to reject were those who disagreed with him on the essentials of the faith (See Day Four of Session Four). They were stirring things up to the point they were causing division, bringing harm to the church. Paul told Titus to warn once, twice, then reject them.

This is a good time for a reminder—we have to be women who know the essentials of the faith so we can recognize when someone is teaching something false.

According to what we've studied, how might you respond to the following scenarios?

- Someone you follow on social media posts that Jesus was not sinless.

- A friend from church wants to discuss whether or not babies should be baptized, communion should only be once a year, or we should only sing hymns.

- A pastor you listen to preaches that God's Word contains error.

- A family member tells you that God requires His people to vote a certain way.

Friends, we have to know when an argument is foolish and unprofitable and when it's not. We also need to be able to identify a divisive person. Knowing the core tenets of our faith will help us recognize the difference between a false teacher and someone just expressing a preference or opinion. So, keep doing what you're doing—study the Bible, listen and learn about the faith, know what you believe!

If Paul warned Titus to avoid certain arguments and reject divisive people, we can surmise that we don't want to be that type of person or be known for the type of argument Titus was to avoid. We need to be careful with our words, not only in what we say about doctrine and theology, but also in how we speak to and about one another.

Ephesians 4:29 was one of the first Bible verses I (Courtney) memorized. It says (I memorized it in the NIV), "Do not let any unwholesome talk come out of your mouths, but only what is helpful for building others up according to their needs, that it may benefit those who listen." Paul wrote these instructions on how God's people should and should not speak.

> Think about the conversations you've had this past week. How would you describe them? Kind, helpful, and necessary? Or critical, foolish, divisive?

Our conversations can go astray in multiple ways. The content or topic can be unprofitable, even harmful. If the majority of our conversations are filled with gossip, slander, or frivolity, then we need to intentionally change how we speak. The actual words we use may be unprofitable. If we use foul language to be funny or add emphasis, our conversations are less profitable—for us and for those listening. And if we are characterized by speaking with sarcasm, anger, or unkind words, then our words will not benefit those who listen.

Spend a few minutes writing down ways your conversations could be more profitable and beneficial. Do you need to focus more on the content of what you talk about, the words you use, or the way you convey your thoughts? Ask God to help you—He will be delighted to!

In verse 14 of our passage, Paul wrote, "Let our people learn to devote themselves to good works for pressing needs, so that they will not be unfruitful." To be devoted means we are so committed to something that it defines our way of life—a habit often practiced and rarely neglected. Notice that Paul wrote this is a learned behavior. It is not who we are naturally.

> In what ways are you devoted to good works? What barriers keep you from a lifestyle of good works?

Joining God in His mission to seek and save the lost requires we believe Him and work to intentionally align our lives with His Word (Col. 4:6). If He says our speech matters, we first have to believe this is true and then work to align our speech with His Word. If God says our lives are most fruitful when we are devoted to good works, we have to first believe this is true and then ask Him to help us devote more and more of our time and resources to the works He calls good.

> How has this passage challenged you? What has been the hardest thing for you to believe from this passage? What's the pressing action you need to take to align yourself with God and His Word? Write a prayer asking God to help you believe and act!

Oh friends, may we each believe God more, be women more aligned with His Word and His ways, women whose speech is characterized by godliness, who are known for good works, and who rest in God's amazing grace.

DAY FIVE

Remind and Review

READ THE WHOLE LETTER TO TITUS.

We've made it to the last day of our study! Oh, how we wish we could all gather around a big table laden with delicious treats and good coffee and take turns sharing what we've learned and how we've encountered the Lord in this study of Titus. That will surely be one of the glories of heaven—sitting together and boasting in all the Lord has done for us.

Let's spend our last day together remembering and reviewing all we've discovered and learned.

> In a sentence or two, how would you summarize Paul's main point(s) in his letter to Titus? In other words, why did Paul write this letter?

I imagine your answer contained words like *grace*, *gospel*, *godliness*, and *good works*. Maybe you mentioned the connections between doctrine and duty or belief and behavior. As a reminder, Paul was writing to encourage Titus to insist on sound doctrine—on the gospel of grace—so that sound churches would be established and the people in those churches would live lives that reflected the gospel they professed. They were to grow in godliness and good works as a result of the gospel of grace!

> In your own words, summarize the gospel of grace. What elements are essential?

SESSION EIGHT: LIVING THE GOSPEL

For this answer, I imagine you included words like *Jesus, kindness, salvation/saved/Savior, hope, righteousness, mercy,* and *eternal life*. Our memory verses will be of great help—for ourselves and others—when we are trying to remember or share the gospel.

Write Titus 3:3-7 from memory.

If you're missing some words or phrases, look at the passage and fill in the missing parts.

Paul certainly had much to say about the local church, especially the character and behavior of the people who make it up.

As a result of this study, what new thoughts do you have about:
- your local church

- the leadership of your church

- the importance of the preaching and teaching in your church

- the concept of church discipline

The church is God's idea. She is not perfect, but is still where God has called us to love, learn, and live in community with others. And is still God's plan to reach the world.

The people in our local churches are who we are to walk through life with. We are called to invest deeply in the lives around us through teaching, encouraging, singing, praying, learning, and pointing each other to Jesus. In other words, you and I are called to lives of discipleship.

> What discipleship relationships are you currently involved in at your church (small group, choir, mission projects, etc.)?

> Are you currently participating in a one-on-one mentoring relationship? If so, what is the dynamic of the relationship? If not, are you compelled to either be discipled or to disciple someone (or both!)?

> Being as specific as possible, what steps will you take towards integrating more discipleship relationships into your life?

By God's grace and the work of the Spirit, He uses both the church and the people who make up the church to transform us. This is how the gospel grows us in godliness.

Part of growing in godliness is growing in Christlike character—and in Titus we've seen that character matters.

> List eight to ten words or phrases from the letter that Paul used to describe godly character. Circle the ones you see currently reflected in your life and underline the ones in which you need to experience growth.

You and I stand down the gospel stream from Paul and Titus. We are recipients of the gospel they believed, guarded, and proclaimed. Now it's our turn! We are called to know, believe, guard, and proclaim. We are called to pass the faith along to the next generation.

Using our session titles, complete each statement with a specific action step. Then use this list as a prayer, asking the Lord to help you walk in godliness and good works.

By God's grace, I will entrust the gospel to others by . . .

_____

By God's grace, I will hold on to the gospel even when it's hard by . . .

_____

By God's grace, I will guard the gospel as I share it with others by . . .

_____

By God's grace, I will adorn the gospel with godliness and good works by . . .

_____

By God's grace, I will believe the gospel by . . .

_____

By God's grace, I will insist on the gospel in my lives and the lives of those around me by . . .

_____

By God's grace, I will live in the gospel of grace by . . .

_____

In Colossians 1:9-10 Paul wrote,

> ⁹ For this reason also, since the day we heard this, we haven't stopped praying for you. We are asking that you may be filled with the knowledge of his will in all wisdom and spiritual understanding, ¹⁰ so that you may walk worthy of the Lord, fully pleasing to him: bearing fruit in every good work and growing in the knowledge of God.

This is our prayer for each of you. And remember, like the book of Titus, everything begins with grace and ends with grace. May we all display that grace more and more in everything we do.

Grace be with all of you!

Singing the Gospel

"Greater Than Our Sin" by Nathan Drake

Session Eight
VIEWER GUIDE

WATCH the Session Eight video teaching and take notes in the space below.

DISCUSSION QUESTIONS

1. What part of Courtney and Hunter's conversation resonated with you the most? Why?

2. Why is it important for you to consider the people in your community of faith as family? Is it easy or difficult for you to do that? Explain. What can you do to foster an atmosphere of family in your church?

3. How have the people in your church been family to you? How have they shown that kind of love, support, and encouragement?

4. Paul warned Titus to avoid foolish debates, quarrels, and disputes. Why do those kinds of things still take place in church? And how can we avoid being drawn into them?

5. Why is discipline sometimes needed in the church family? How can this be done in a healthy, redemptive way?

6. There is unity in the message of the gospel and diversity in how we accomplish the mission of making disciples through the gospel. What do you see as your part in the mission? How are you using your gifts and skills to make disciples?

7. How does this passage call you to display the gospel of grace?

8. How has this study affected the way you see the church and your place in it?

9. What is your main takeaway from this study and how will you apply it? Use your insights from the list on p. 162 to help you answer.

 To access the video teaching sessions, use the instructions in the back of your Bible study book.

ENDNOTES

Session Two

1. David Platt, Daniel L. Akin, Tony Merida, *Christ-Centered Exposition Commentary: Exalting Jesus in 1 & 2 Timothy and Titus* (B&H Publishing Group, 2013), 229.

Session Three

1. Tim Chester, *Titus for You* (The Good Book Co., 2014), 31.

Session Four

1. *ESV Archaeology Study Bible* (Crossway, 2018), Note on Titus 1:12-13.

2. Brennan Manning; DC Talk, "What if I Stumble?," *Jesus Freak*, Virgin Records, 1995.

3. Merriam-Webster's Unabridged Dictionary, "Tertiary," accessed November 11, 2024, https://unabridged.merriam-webster.com/unabridged/tertiary.

Session Six

1. D. A. Carson, *For the Love of God*, volume 2 (Intervarsity Press, 1999), January 23rd entry.

Session Seven

1. David Garner, "The Holy Spirit: Agent of Salvation," The Gospel Coalition, accessed Nov. 11, 2024, https://www.thegospelcoalition.org/essay/the-holy-spirit-agent-of-salvation/.

Session Eight

1. Matt Schmucker, "Something Different," Ligonier Ministries, March 1, 2009, https://www.ligonier.org/learn/articles/something-different.

2. Cyprian, "The Treatises of Cyprian: Treatise I: On the Unity of the Church," *Ante-Nicene Fathers*, Volume 5, Ed. Philip Schaff, Christian Classics Ethereal Library, accessed November 11, 2024, https://www.ccel.org/ccel/schaff/anf05.iv.v.i.html.

GLOSSARY

APOSTLE: The New Testament primarily uses the word apostle to refer to the twelve disciples and Paul—men who had seen the risen Christ and been commissioned by him to preach the gospel to the ends of the earth.

CHURCH DISCIPLINE: The act of excluding someone who professes to be a Christian from membership in the church and participation in the Lord's Supper for serious unrepentant sin—sin they refuse to let go of.

CROSS REFERENCE: Another verse in the Bible that shares a similar word, topic, or theme with the verse you are reading.

DISCIPLE (NOUN): One who follows Jesus.

DISCIPLE (VERB): To teach and model how to follow Jesus.

DISCIPLESHIP: Teaching and training in godliness in the context of relationship.

DOCTRINE: Teaching that aligns with Scripture and results in godly living.

ELDER: One who oversees and manages the affairs of the local church. In Scripture, the words elder, pastor, and overseer are often used to reference the same office.

GRACE: God's unmerited favor.

IMPERATIVE: A command or order.

INDICATIVE: A true statement.

ORTHODOX: At its core, the word means right belief. Orthodoxy consists in the historical faith, summarized in the early creeds like the Apostles' Creed and the Nicene Creed.

PEACE: A complete sense of well-being in and through Christ.

SANCTIFICATION: The lifelong process of being increasingly conformed to Jesus's righteousness through the work of the Holy Spirit.

SOUND: Healthy, whole, fully functioning, not broken.

Notes

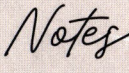

Notes

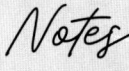

THE GOSPEL DOESN'T JUST CHANGE YOUR ETERNAL FUTURE; IT CHANGES YOUR PRESENT REALITY.

In this 9-session study on the book of Romans, Courtney Doctor will walk you through Paul's powerful letter to see the glorious grace and transforming work of the gospel. You'll be overwhelmed with the good news of God's merciful rescue as you better understand the depth of your need. This life-changing message provides not only hope for eternity, but purpose, joy, and peace for today. And as the good news of the gospel of grace unfolds through Romans, it will compel you to proclaim God's glorious salvation to all.

Bible Study Book with
Video Access 005833030 $21.99
DVD Set 005836158 $49.99

lifeway.com/mercies | 800.458.2772

Lifeway women

Pricing and availability are subject to change without notice.

Also available for kids from **Hunter Beless**

Available wherever books are sold!

Lifeway women
ACADEMY

Online courses for women, by women.

Are you curious about how to study the Bible more deeply and apply it to your daily life? Lifeway Women Academy offers courses on topics like practical ministry, historical and cultural context, and theology, to help you grow in your understanding of God's Word and gain confidence in sharing it with others.

If you're interested in learning how to study and teach the Bible on your own, how to make disciples at home and everywhere you go, and how you can use your gifts for the kingdom, Lifeway Women Academy is where you begin.

WITH LIFEWAY WOMEN ACADEMY, YOU WILL:

- Get on-demand courses you can complete at your own pace.
- Grow in your understanding of what the Bible says and how to study it faithfully.
- Gain confidence and competence in studying God's Word and leading others to do the same.
- Be equipped with knowledge and practical steps to love God and make disciples.

Learn from trusted teachers like:
Jen Wilkin, Elizabeth Woodson, and **Courtney Doctor**

DISCOVER AVAILABLE COURSES

The Handbook SERIES

Elegantly designed for deep study and lifelong discipleship.

Immerse yourself in the Handbook Series, elegant, full-color Bible handbooks that include robust summary content, charts, maps, word studies, illustrations, and more for every book of the Bible. Constructed with high-quality cloth cover materials and a sewn binding, these handbooks are designed to last a lifetime as valuable companion resources for Bible study, teaching, and ongoing discipleship.

HOLMAN® REFERENCE

SCAN TO SHOP NOW

Get the most from your study.

Customize your Bible study time with a guided experience.

In this study you'll:

- Study Titus verse by verse to learn to believe, portray, and proclaim the gospel
- Understand how the gospel transforms lives, churches, and communities
- Discover how important sound doctrine is to the integrity and proclamation of the gospel
- Embrace the impact your character and conduct have on your witness

STUDYING ON YOUR OWN?

Watch Courtney Doctor and Hunter Beless's teaching sessions, available via redemption code for individual video-streaming access, printed in this Bible study book.

LEADING A GROUP?

Each group member will need a *Titus* Bible study book, which includes video access. Because all participants will have access to the video content, you can choose to watch the videos outside of your group meeting if desired. Or, if you're watching together and someone misses a group meeting, they'll have the flexibility to catch up! A DVD set is also available to purchase separately if desired.

ALSO AVAILABLE

DVD Set, includes 8 video teaching sessions from Courtney Doctor and Hunter Beless, each approximately 25-30 minutes.

Ebook with video access, includes 8 video teaching sessions from Courtney Doctor and Hunter Beless, each approximately 25-30 minutes.

Browse study formats, a free session sample, leader guide, video clips, church promotional materials, and more at

lifeway.com/titus

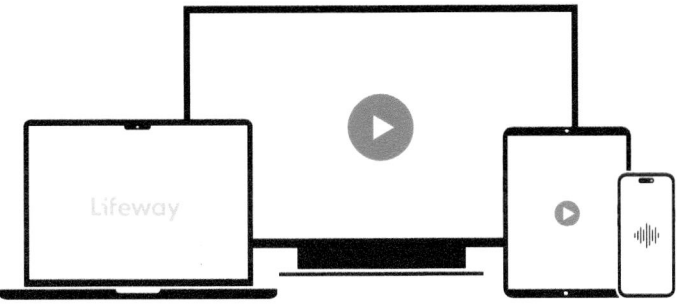

HERE'S YOUR VIDEO ACCESS.

You're just a few steps away from viewing your *Titus* Bible study teaching sessions.

1. Go to **my.lifeway.com/redeem** and register or log in to your Lifeway account.
2. Enter the redemption code below to unlock your video access:

YBC4D6BJKP8G

Once you've entered your personal redemption code, you can stream the video teaching sessions using the Lifeway On Demand app. Watch on your phone or tablet or cast to your TV. These sessions will also appear in your Lifeway account at my.lifeway.com.

 Want to listen on the go? Play your video through the Lifeway On Demand app, lock your screen, and enjoy the audio teaching like a podcast.

QUESTIONS? WE HAVE ANSWERS!
Visit **support.lifeway.com** and search "Video Redemption Code" or call our Tech Support Team at 866.627.8553.

This video access code entitles you to one non-transferable, single-seat license with no expiration date. Please do not share your code with others. Videos are subject to expiration at the discretion of the publisher. Do not post Bible study videos to YouTube, Vimeo, any social media channel, or other online services for any purpose. Such posting constitutes copyright infringement and is prohibited by the terms of use. Unauthorized posting also violates the service rules, which can negatively affect your YouTube or other service account.